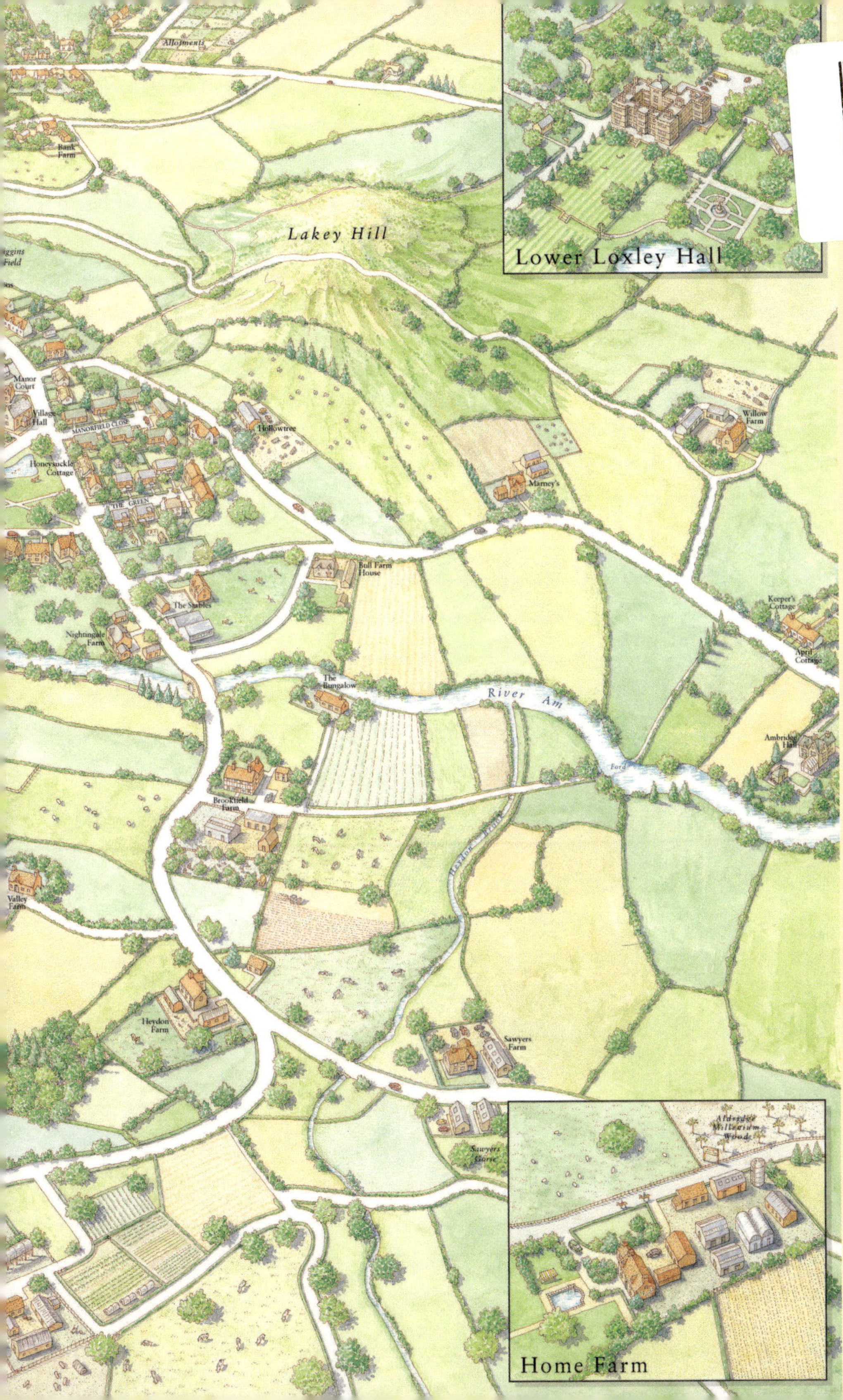
Allotments
Bank Farm
Lakey Hill
Lower Loxley Hall
Manor Court
Village Hall
Manorfield Close
Hollowtree
Willow Farm
Marney's
Honeysuckle Cottage
The Green
Bull Farm House
The Stables
Nightingale Farm
Keeper's Cottage
April Cottage
The Bungalow
River Am
Ambridge Hall
Ford
Brookfield Farm
Heydon Brook
Valley Farm
Heydon Farm
Sawyers Farm
Sawyers Gorse
Aldridge Millennium Wood
Home Farm

The Archers
DIARY 2009

F

FRANCES LINCOLN LIMITED
PUBLISHERS

Frances Lincoln Limited
4 Torriano Mews
Torriano Avenue
London NW5 2RZ
www.franceslincoln.com

The Archers Diary 2009

Copyright © Frances Lincoln Limited 2008
Text copyright © Hedli Niklaus 2008
All photographs copyright © John Eveson 2008 except the front and back cover, pages 1, 6–7, 14, 16, 71 and 107 and weeks 1, 11, 17, 24, 30, 35, 44, 46, 52.

Photos of the cast are by permission of BBC Picture Publicity and are BBC copyright.

The Archers logo copyright © BBC 1998
The BBC Radio Four logo copyright © BBC 2000
Licensed by BBC Worldwide Ltd
The Archers and Ambridge word mark and logo and the BBC Radio Four word mark and logo are trade marks of the British Broacasting Corporation and are used under License. All characters and place names are associated with the BBC Radio Four series The Archers.
Photographs on front cover and p. 14 © James Kerr
Ambridge panorama map © Magnetic North

Astronomical information © Crown Copyright. Reproduced by permission of the Controller of Her Majesty's Stationery Office and the UK Hydrographic Office (www.ukho.gov.uk)

All rights reserved. No part of this publication may be reproduced, stored in a retrieval system or transmitted, in any form, or by any means, electronic, mechanical, photocopying, recording or otherwise, without either prior permission in writing from the publishers or a licence permitting restricted copying. In the United Kingdom such licences are issued by the Copyright Licensing Agency, Saffron House, 6–10 Kirby Street, London, EC1N 8TS.

British Library cataloguing-in-publication data
A catalogue record for this book is available from the British Library

ISBN: 978-0-7112-2846-7

Printed in China

First Frances Lincoln edition 2008

ACKNOWLEDGMENTS
The Publisher would like to thank Vanessa Whitburn, Editor of The Archers, and Kate Oates, Producer, for their contribution. Thanks also to Kate Tanner, Archers Archivist Camilla Fisher and to Dominic Beddow of Magnetic North and Archers Addicts for permission to use The Ambridge Panorama.

ARCHERS ADDICTS
Archers Addicts is the Official Fan Club for BBC Radio 4's The Archers. For further details and a colour brochure, please contact PO Box 1951, Stratford-upon-Avon, Warwickshire, CV37 1YH
Telephone: 01789 207470
www.archers-addicts.com

Back cover (from left to right): DORIS ARCHER (GWEN BERRYMAN), DAN ARCHER (HARRY OAKES), CHRISTINE ARCHER (LESLEY SAWEARD), PHIL ARCHER (NORMAN PAINTING)

Title page (from left to right): NED LARKIN (BILL PAYNE), PAUL JOHNSON (LESLIE DUNN), JIMMY GRANGE (ALAN ROTHWELL)

CALENDAR 2009

JANUARY
M	T	W	T	F	S	S
			1	2	3	4
5	6	7	8	9	10	11
12	13	14	15	16	17	18
19	20	21	22	23	24	25
26	27	28	29	30	31	

FEBRUARY
M	T	W	T	F	S	S
						1
2	3	4	5	6	7	8
9	10	11	12	13	14	15
16	17	18	19	20	21	22
23	24	25	26	27	28	

MARCH
M	T	W	T	F	S	S
						1
2	3	4	5	6	7	8
9	10	11	12	13	14	15
16	17	18	19	20	21	22
23	24	25	26	27	28	29
30	31					

APRIL
M	T	W	T	F	S	S
		1	2	3	4	5
6	7	8	9	10	11	12
13	14	15	16	17	18	19
20	21	22	23	24	25	26
27	28	29	30			

MAY
M	T	W	T	F	S	S
				1	2	3
4	5	6	7	8	9	10
11	12	13	14	15	16	17
18	19	20	21	22	23	24
25	26	27	28	29	30	31

JUNE
M	T	W	T	F	S	S
1	2	3	4	5	6	7
8	9	10	11	12	13	14
15	16	17	18	19	20	21
22	23	24	25	26	27	28
29	30					

JULY
M	T	W	T	F	S	S
		1	2	3	4	5
6	7	8	9	10	11	12
13	14	15	16	17	18	19
20	21	22	23	24	25	26
27	28	29	30	31		

AUGUST
M	T	W	T	F	S	S
					1	2
3	4	5	6	7	8	9
10	11	12	13	14	15	16
17	18	19	20	21	22	23
24	25	26	27	28	29	30
31						

SEPTEMBER
M	T	W	T	F	S	S
	1	2	3	4	5	6
7	8	9	10	11	12	13
14	15	16	17	18	19	20
21	22	23	24	25	26	27
28	29	30				

OCTOBER
M	T	W	T	F	S	S
			1	2	3	4
5	6	7	8	9	10	11
12	13	14	15	16	17	18
19	20	21	22	23	24	25
26	27	28	29	30	31	

NOVEMBER
M	T	W	T	F	S	S
						1
2	3	4	5	6	7	8
9	10	11	12	13	14	15
16	17	18	19	20	21	22
23	24	25	26	27	28	29
30						

DECEMBER
M	T	W	T	F	S	S
	1	2	3	4	5	6
7	8	9	10	11	12	13
14	15	16	17	18	19	20
21	22	23	24	25	26	27
28	29	30	31			

CALENDAR 2010

JANUARY
M	T	W	T	F	S	S
				1	2	3
4	5	6	7	8	9	10
11	12	13	14	15	16	17
18	19	20	21	22	23	24
25	26	27	28	29	30	31

FEBRUARY
M	T	W	T	F	S	S
1	2	3	4	5	6	7
8	9	10	11	12	13	14
15	16	17	18	19	20	21
22	23	24	25	26	27	

MARCH
M	T	W	T	F	S	S
1	2	3	4	5	6	7
8	9	10	11	12	13	14
15	16	17	18	19	20	21
22	23	24	25	26	27	28
29	30	31				

APRIL
M	T	W	T	F	S	S
			1	2	3	4
5	6	7	8	9	10	11
12	13	14	15	16	17	18
19	20	21	22	23	24	25
26	27	28	29	30		

MAY
M	T	W	T	F	S	S
					1	2
3	4	5	6	7	8	9
10	11	12	13	14	15	16
17	18	19	20	21	22	23
24	25	26	27	28	29	30
31						

JUNE
M	T	W	T	F	S	S
	1	2	3	4	5	6
7	8	9	10	11	12	13
14	15	16	17	18	19	20
21	22	23	24	25	26	27
28	29	30				

JULY
M	T	W	T	F	S	S
			1	2	3	4
5	6	7	8	9	10	11
12	13	14	15	16	17	18
19	20	21	22	23	24	25
26	27	28	29	30	31	

AUGUST
M	T	W	T	F	S	S
						1
2	3	4	5	6	7	8
9	10	11	12	13	14	15
16	17	18	19	20	21	22
23	24	25	26	27	28	29
30	31					

SEPTEMBER
M	T	W	T	F	S	S
		1	2	3	4	5
6	7	8	9	10	11	12
13	14	15	16	17	18	19
20	21	22	23	24	25	26
27	28	29	30			

OCTOBER
M	T	W	T	F	S	S
				1	2	3
4	5	6	7	8	9	10
11	12	13	14	15	16	17
18	19	20	21	22	23	24
25	26	27	28	29	30	31

NOVEMBER
M	T	W	T	F	S	S
1	2	3	4	5	6	7
8	9	10	11	12	13	14
15	16	17	18	19	20	21
22	23	24	25	26	27	28
29	30					

DECEMBER
M	T	W	T	F	S	S
		1	2	3	4	5
6	7	8	9	10	11	12
13	14	15	16	17	18	19
20	21	22	23	24	25	26
27	28	29	30	31		

INTRODUCTION

You know what they say in the property industry: 'Location, location, location', and where would *The Archers* be without Ambridge and its environs? This is why, in the *Archers Diary 2009*, we have decided to focus on some of our favourite places in Ambridge; places that have set the scene for love, jealousy, angst and delight. From Nigel and Elizabeth's decision to go green at Lower Loxley, fights over pews at St. Stephen's, cordon-bleu catering at Grey Gables, and proposals and heartbreak on Lakey Hill, Ambridge would be nothing without its solitary and social spaces.

It's true that there are as many versions of Ambridge as there are listeners, and we invite you to compare your image of Ambridge with ours; take our quiz to determine exactly how much you know about the village, and enjoy exquisite pictures that present you with a beautiful world of nature, village life, key events, and the changing seasons. And as the seasons pass, no matter where you live, you can carry a piece of Ambridge with you! So join us in celebrating the best storylines, delights and dramas of Ambridge village life - if only the walls could talk, they'd give Lynda Snell a run for her money!

Archers Addicts
Official fan club for BBC Radio 4's *The Archers*
www.archers-addicts.com

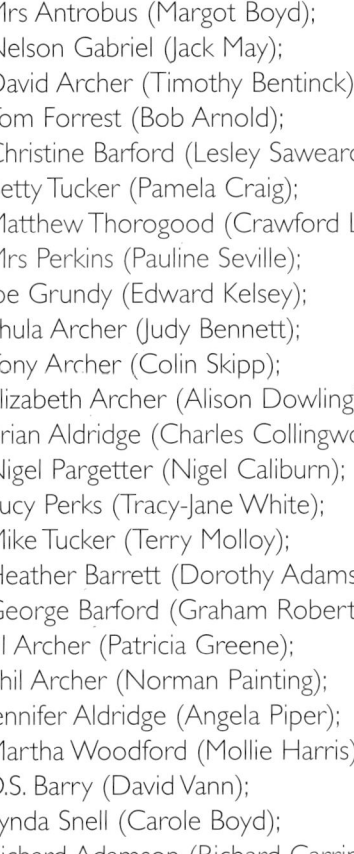

Publicity picture, 1985
From left to right, character name followed by name of actor in brackets:
Eddie Grundy (Trevor Harrison);
Pat Archer (Patricia Gallimore);
Mark Hebden (Richard Derrington);
Clarrie Grundy (Fiona Mathieson);
Neil Carter (Brian Hewlett);
Sophie Barlow (Moir Leslie);
Colonel Danby (Ballard Berkeley);
Mrs Antrobus (Margot Boyd);
Nelson Gabriel (Jack May);
David Archer (Timothy Bentinck);
Tom Forrest (Bob Arnold);
Christine Barford (Lesley Saweard);
Betty Tucker (Pamela Craig);
Matthew Thorogood (Crawford Logan);
Mrs Perkins (Pauline Seville);
Joe Grundy (Edward Kelsey);
Shula Archer (Judy Bennett);
Tony Archer (Colin Skipp);
Elizabeth Archer (Alison Dowling);
Brian Aldridge (Charles Collingwood);
Nigel Pargetter (Nigel Caliburn);
Lucy Perks (Tracy-Jane White);
Mike Tucker (Terry Molloy);
Heather Barrett (Dorothy Adamson);
George Barford (Graham Roberts);
Jill Archer (Patricia Greene);
Phil Archer (Norman Painting);
Jennifer Aldridge (Angela Piper);
Martha Woodford (Mollie Harris);
D.S. Barry (David Vann);
Lynda Snell (Carole Boyd);
Richard Adamson (Richard Carrington);
Caroline Bone (Sara Coward);
Jack Woolley (Arnold Peters);
Peggy Archer (June Spencer);
Walter Gabriel (Chris Gittins);
Robert Snell (Graham Blockey);
Kathy Holland (Hedli Niklaus);
Sid Perks (Alan Devereux);
Susan Carter (Charlotte Martin).

BIRTHDAYS AND ANNIVERSARIES

You can record whether you share special dates with those in Ambridge, as well as Archers gift ideas so that you are not stuck for inspiration when the time comes.

JANUARY

APRIL

FEBRUARY

MAY

MARCH

JUNE

JULY

AUGUST

SEPTEMBER

CHRISTMAS

OCTOBER

NOVEMBER

DECEMBER

THE ULTIMATE CONTACT SHEET

FAMILY

Name .... Name .... Name .... Name ....
H .... H .... H .... H ....
W .... W .... W .... W ....
M .... M .... M .... M ....

Name .... Name .... Name .... Name ....
H .... H .... H .... H ....
W .... W .... W .... W ....
M .... M .... M .... M ....

WORK CONTACTS

NEIGHBOURS   DOCTOR   DENTIST

OPTICIAN   HOSPITAL   POLICE STATION   LOCAL COUNCIL

BANKS

BUILDING SOCIETIES

MORTGAGE LENDER/LANDLORD

FAVOURITE RESTAURANTS/TAKEAWAYS

OTHER USEFUL NUMBERS

USEFUL LINKS

BBC Radio 4 – Official BBC Archers site, includes a listen-again facility and podcast download:
www.bbc.co.uk/radio4/archers

Archers Addicts – Official fan club for *The Archers*, featuring the Village Shop, on-line fan club newspaper, competitions, Ambridge gossip, shop and forums:
www.archers-addicts.com

ACTORS' SITES

Timothy Bentinck (David Archer) features a personal site crammed with information about all his other interests and work besides *The Archers*: www.bentinck.net

Terry Molloy (Mike Tucker) has a site which combines Ambridge with *Dr Who* (hear Davros!): www.terrymolloy.co.uk

BORSETSHIRE BRAINTEASERS

So you never miss an episode, but how well do you really know your way around Ambridge? Solve these puzzles to find out whether you're a Scout leader or hopeless hiker! Solutions are on page 128 so, if you can find them without a compass, check your answers and read your rating. Good luck (and don't forget your Kendal mint cake)!

RAMBLING AMBRIDGE ANAGRAMS!

Let's stretch your legs with a few quick anagrams. Re-arrange the letters below to discover six key Ambridge locations. Each answer consists of two words.

Thespians Nest
Reel Lowly Ox
Barley Eggs
A Hilly Elk
Bell Hut
Offer Broad Milk

LOST IN SPACE!

Where are you? One drink too many at The Bull can make it hard to find your way home (ask Eddie!). Change one letter in each of the words below to arrive safely!

Here's an example to help you warm-up!
Prey Cables = **G**rey **G**ables

Granie Warm
Polite Horse
Woodbike Dottage
Pillage Hull
Moneysuckle Coltage
Nightinjale Firm
She Staples
Umbridge Wall
Beeper's Cotgage
Pillow Barm

GUESS WHO?

Solve the clues to reveal the surnames of ten of our favourite Ambridge families, then find them in the word search opposite. There are a few letters in each clue to help you on your way and give yourself a point for every answer you get right. Here's an easy one to get you going…

1. This chap's done **sterling** work saving his dairy.
2. On a **par** with country gentlemen everywhere, this man has a penchant for wine.
3. This girl bi**cker**s with her brother, but they've pulled together since the birth of his second child.
4. This is an **arch**etypal Ambridge family who are essential to the show!
5. This man loves a good Harvest Supper and gives his th**anks** before every meal.
6. A budding farrier, this fellow needs a filly to pull his **cart**!
7. This long-suffering lady's cakes are renowned throughout the village, but she keeps the recipes **und**er wraps.
8. This woman's been through a few surnames but remained **loy**al to the chap that gave her this one, even when he took a gamble with their finances!
9. Once an Archer, this lady swapped one Jack for another and she keeps warm with a lovely **wool**ly jumper.
10. One of the **perks** of this man's job is being his own boss and lording it over his customers!

F	S	R	E	G	H	A	W	T	O	O	L	A	P	S	R	K	J
W	L	C	S	T	E	R	L	I	N	G	R	S	Y	E	Y	O	P
O	T	G	Y	J	K	H	L	B	Y	E	M	E	T	H	Z	K	G
G	O	V	T	O	E	C	O	W	U	I	H	R	U	X	H	S	N
P	R	G	R	U	N	D	Y	P	R	D	A	L	D	G	T	A	D
E	I	Y	E	G	T	A	D	W	S	C	J	S	A	R	E	R	L
A	R	E	T	F	C	R	L	N	O	F	U	P	E	N	P	C	Y
G	C	S	U	M	Q	G	S	E	N	P	W	T	G	Y	A	H	W
T	H	O	C	E	W	A	R	K	M	I	D	N	I	R	S	E	K
R	W	Y	K	A	T	O	Z	Y	N	O	P	R	S	V	T	R	C
R	L	B	E	P	K	R	O	R	S	A	E	K	L	T	A	E	L
Y	K	N	R	H	I	R	S	H	S	B	R	P	E	L	O	C	R
N	E	S	D	O	K	T	W	T	L	E	G	F	N	A	H	U	T
D	R	L	T	U	C	A	J	R	P	E	M	K	P	S	Q	H	S
O	M	O	L	Y	T	P	X	U	D	Y	T	F	O	L	Y	D	I
R	S	Y	U	O	K	L	E	P	A	R	G	E	T	T	E	R	T
G	A	T	T	G	O	R	G	O	W	U	D	A	R	Y	O	L	O
P	A	R	N	D	S	W	L	R	E	S	G	N	I	T	Y	N	W

HOW DID YOU SCORE? (answers on page 128)

🏆🏆🏆🏆 21–26
Congratulations! Lace up your walking boots and throw away your compass – you know the bumps and furrows of Ambridge land as well as Phil Archer.

🏆🏆🏆 14–20
Well done! Jennifer would find your help invaluable and her website would zing! Your knowledge is built on stone as strong as the foundations of Grey Gables.

🏆🏆 7–13
Could do better! Cling on to that map and take supplies – you're as hapless as a sheep in fog and will be lost in Heydon Wood before you know it.

🏆 0–6
Oh dear! Your brain is as open and vacant as the rolling landscape of Lakey Hill (or Eddie Grundy's). At least there it's calm and quiet.

AMBRIDGE LANDMARKS
St. Stephen's Church

THE DETAILS:

Location: South of the River Am
Age: Built on the site of a seventh-century Augustinian Church and consecrated in 1281
Style: Late Norman and Early English styles
Facilities: Set of bells and a working clock with mechanical chime
Staff: Vicar: Alan Franks; Church warden: Bert Fry; Captain of Bell Ringers: Neil Carter; Organist: Phil Archer.

CHURCH PEWS & NEWS:

St. Stephen's is one of the oldest landmarks in Ambridge. During building work in 1992, ancient foundations were discovered and carbon dating revealed that timbers in the church tower were Saxon, dating from between 540–560 AD. The church has all the common problems with upkeep that beset churches today. Once there were so many mice that Tom Forrest hurled a handy hymn book in their direction: nothing daunted they continued to chew through the leather organ stops, preventing Phil from playing the organ on Sundays.

Current incumbent, Alan Franks (John Telfer) see right, dressed in his leathers and weaving about Ambridge on his motor bike, keeps everyone on their toes with his passionate commitment to his job. Fortunately Alan's prayers to reach earth safely were heard when, in 2007, he scaled the dizzy heights of the Church tower and abseiled from it in order to raise money for charity.

As with so many churches St Stephen's has marked key events in the lives of many Ambridge villagers, especially those of the Archer family. One of St Stephen's most prized features is the stained glass window donated by George Fairbrother in 1959, in memory of his daughter, Grace Archer.

IF WALLS HAD EARS…

- …they'd ring with the sound of raised voices when Ambridge's first female Vicar, Janet Fisher, was ordained in 1995. Peggy Woolley, among others, was so outraged at the prospect she moved her alliance to the All Saints Church in Borchester.

- …they'd know that St Mary's in Hanbury, Worcestershire is the church that acts as a model for St Stephen's in real life, and has been used in publicity pictures since the series started in 1951 (see opposite page). Fans of the programme still journey to see where David and Ruth were 'married' and Dan and Doris 'buried'.

- …they'd be surprised to hear the church clock strike after several years of silence. The wealthy Jack Woolley and Cameron Fraser battled it out to pay for the clock repairs but sadly, soon after its first chime, the weights crashed through the floor nearly crushing William Grundy on the way down.

 **SOUNDBITE:**
The two bells hung most recently in the bell tower of St. Stephen's are dedicated: 'In Memory of Tom Forrest – Bell-ringer and Tower Captain, and his devoted wife, Pru.' Tom and Pru Forrest were one of Ambridge's most devoted couples and died within a week of each other in 1998. Pictured right are Tom Forrest (Bob Arnold), Walter Gabriel (Chris Gittins) and Dan Archer (Harry Oakes).

DECEMBER|JANUARY

WEEK 1
2009

29 Monday

30 Tuesday

31 Wednesday

New Year's Eve
JOHN ARCHER BORN 1975

1 Thursday

New Year's Day
Holiday, UK, Republic of Ireland, Canada, USA,
Australia and New Zealand
JACK AND PEGGY WOOLLEY MARRIED 1991
***THE ARCHERS* FIRST BROADCAST NATIONWIDE 1951**

2 Friday

Holiday, Scotland and New Zealand

3 Saturday

4 Sunday

First Quarter

JACK AND PEGGY WOOLLEY (ARNOLD PETERS AND JUNE SPENCER)

JANUARY

WEEK 2
2009

5 Monday

6 Tuesday   *Epiphany*

7 Wednesday   JENNIFER ALDRIDGE BORN 1945

8 Thursday

9 Friday

10 Saturday   PAT ARCHER BORN 1952

11 Sunday   *Full Moon*

JANUARY

WEEK 3
2009

12 Monday

13 Tuesday

14 Wednesday

15 Thursday

16 Friday

17 Saturday   GEORGE BARFORD DIED 2005

18 Sunday   *Last Quarter*

JANUARY

WEEK 4
2009

19 Monday Holiday, USA (Martin Luther King's Birthday)
NOLUTHANDO MADIKANE BORN 2001

20 Tuesday

21 Wednesday BRENDA TUCKER BORN 1981

22 Thursday

23 Friday

24 Saturday

25 Sunday

DAN ARCHER (EDGAR HARRISON) SHAKES HANDS WITH THE VICAR AS AMBRIDGE VILLAGERS LEAVE ST. STEPHEN'S CHURCH.

JANUARY | FEBRUARY

WEEK 5
2009

26 Monday

Chinese New Year
Holiday, Australia (Australia Day)
New Moon

27 Tuesday

28 Wednesday

29 Thursday

30 Friday

KATHY PERKS BORN 1953

31 Saturday

1 Sunday

FEBRUARY

WEEK 6
2009

2 Monday

First Quarter
ROY TUCKER BORN 1978

3 Tuesday

4 Wednesday

5 Thursday

6 Friday

Holiday, New Zealand (Waitangi Day)
Accession of Queen Elizabeth II

7 Saturday

8 Sunday

FEBRUARY

WEEK 7
2009

9 Monday

Full Moon
WILLIAM GRUNDY BORN 1983

10 Tuesday

11 Wednesday

12 Thursday

Holiday, USA (Lincoln's Birthday)

13 Friday

14 Saturday

St. Valentine's Day

15 Sunday

FEBRUARY

WEEK 8
2009

16 Monday

Holiday, USA (Washington's Birthday)
Last Quarter
TONY ARCHER BORN 1951

17 Tuesday

PIP ARCHER BORN 1993
MARK HEBDEN DIED 1994

18 Wednesday

19 Thursday

20 Friday

MARK HEBDEN BORN 1955

21 Saturday

22 Sunday

FEBRUARY | MARCH

WEEK 9
2009

23 Monday

24 Tuesday • Shrove Tuesday

25 Wednesday
Ash Wednesday
New Moon
TOM ARCHER BORN 1981
NEIL AND SUSAN CARTER MARRIED 1984
JOHN ARCHER DIED 1998

26 Thursday

27 Friday

28 Saturday

1 Sunday
St. David's Day
CHRISTINE AND GEORGE BARFORD MARRIED 1979

ST. STEPHEN'S CHURCH

SWEET TREATS
AUNTIE SATYA'S MODAK

Usha has spiced up Rev. Alan Frank's life no end, not least with her cooking. Soon after arriving in Ambridge, Marjorie Antrobus wrongly assumed Usha was a natural in the kitchen and got her talking to the WI on 'A Taste of India' with predictable results. However, Usha's cooking has improved over the years, largely under the influence of Auntie Satya. Why not sweeten your friends and family with this tasty little number? Alan recommends it.

Serves a crowd!

INGREDIENTS

For the dough:
1kg (2lb 3oz) powdered sugar (icing sugar)
1kg (2lb 3oz) khoya (see Top Tip)
A pinch of cardamom powder

For the filling:
100g (4oz) almonds, finely chopped
100g (4oz) pistachios, finely chopped
200g (8oz) sugar

METHOD

- Add the icing sugar and cardamom powder to the khoya.
- Mix together and knead into a soft dough.
- Mix the pistachios, almonds and sugar.
- Lightly grease your palms and form some of the dough into a small ball.
- Make a hollow in the middle of the ball, and place about a teaspoonful of the almond and pistachio mixture inside.
- Carefully pull up the sides and gather them at the top, giving your sweet a conical shape, or the shape of a fig.

☆ USHA'S TOP TIP ☆

"If, like me, you struggle to get hold of khoya, just use ricotta cheese instead. Pan fry it over a medium heat until it loses all the water content and becomes a dark yellow in colour. Or, if you haven't got the time to make it yourself, just ask Auntie Satya!"

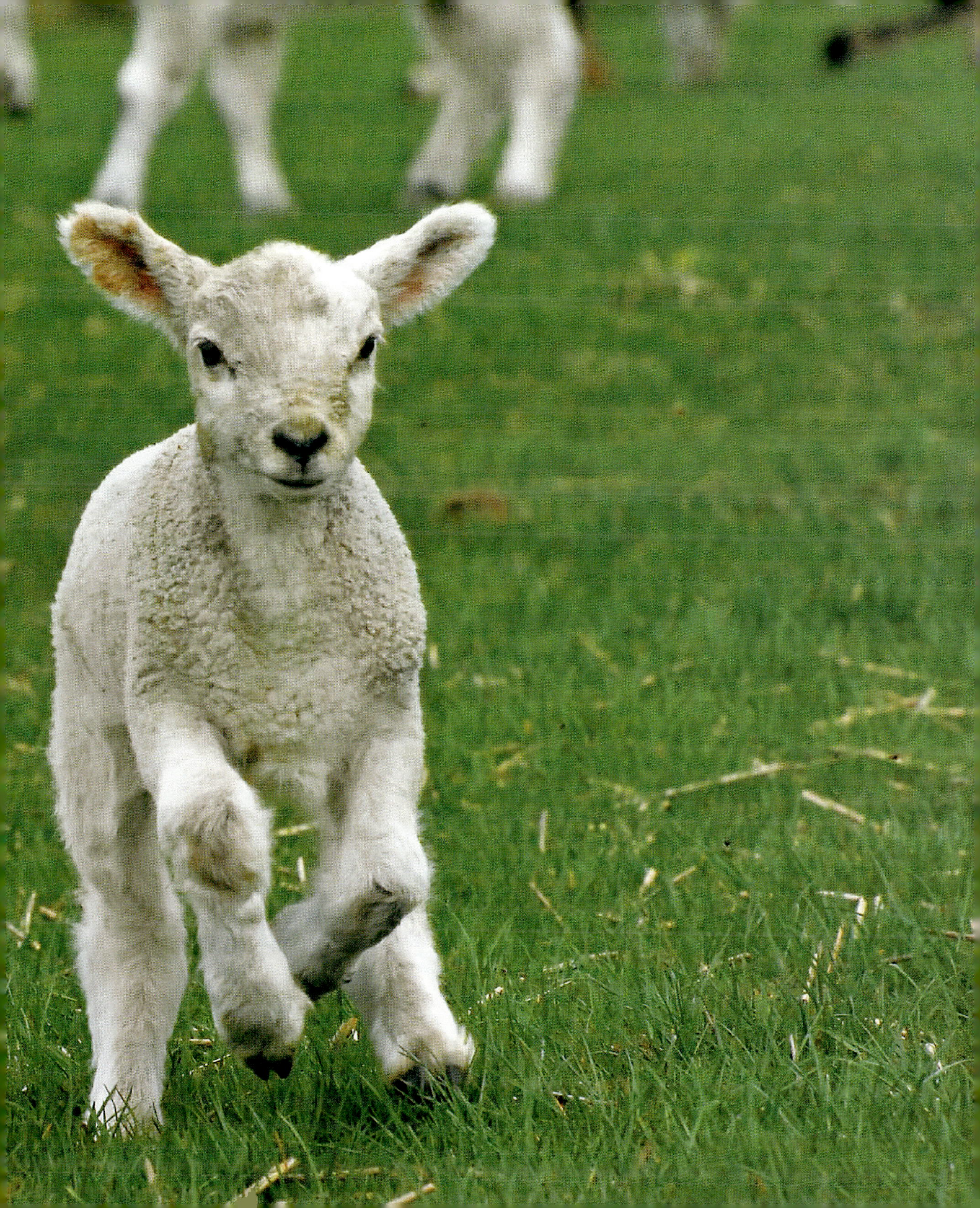

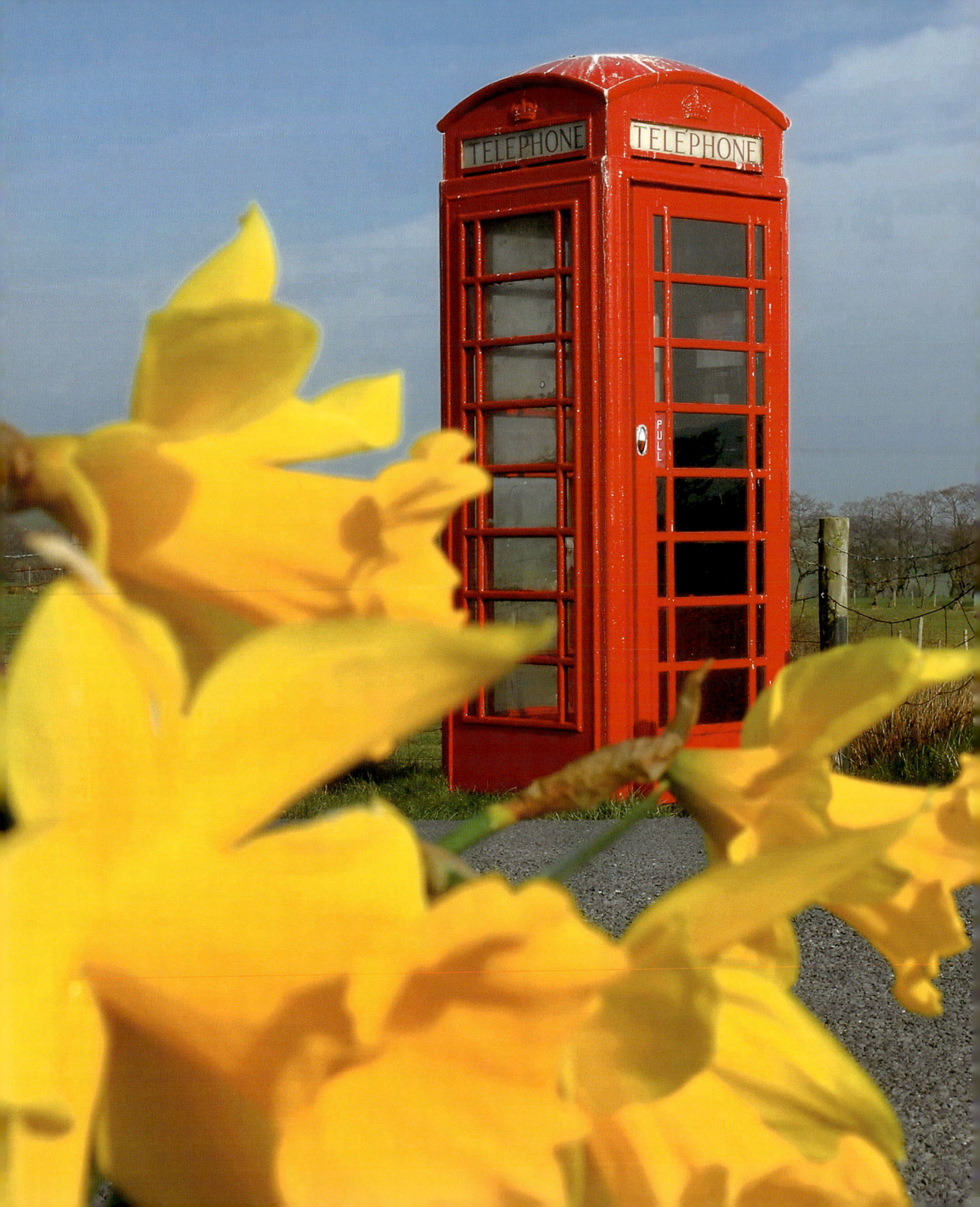
TELEPHONE
TELEPHONE
PULL

MARCH

WEEK 10
2009

2 Monday

3 Tuesday

4 Wednesday *First Quarter*

5 Thursday

6 Friday

7 Saturday ABIGAIL TUCKER BORN 2008

8 Sunday

MARCH

WEEK 11
2009

9 Monday Commonwealth Day

10 Tuesday

11 Wednesday *Full Moon*

12 Thursday

13 Friday

14 Saturday

15 Sunday EDDIE GRUNDY BORN 1951
BENJAMIN ARCHER BORN 2002

EDDIE AND CLARRIE GRUNDY (TREVOR HARRISON AND ROSALIND ADAMS)

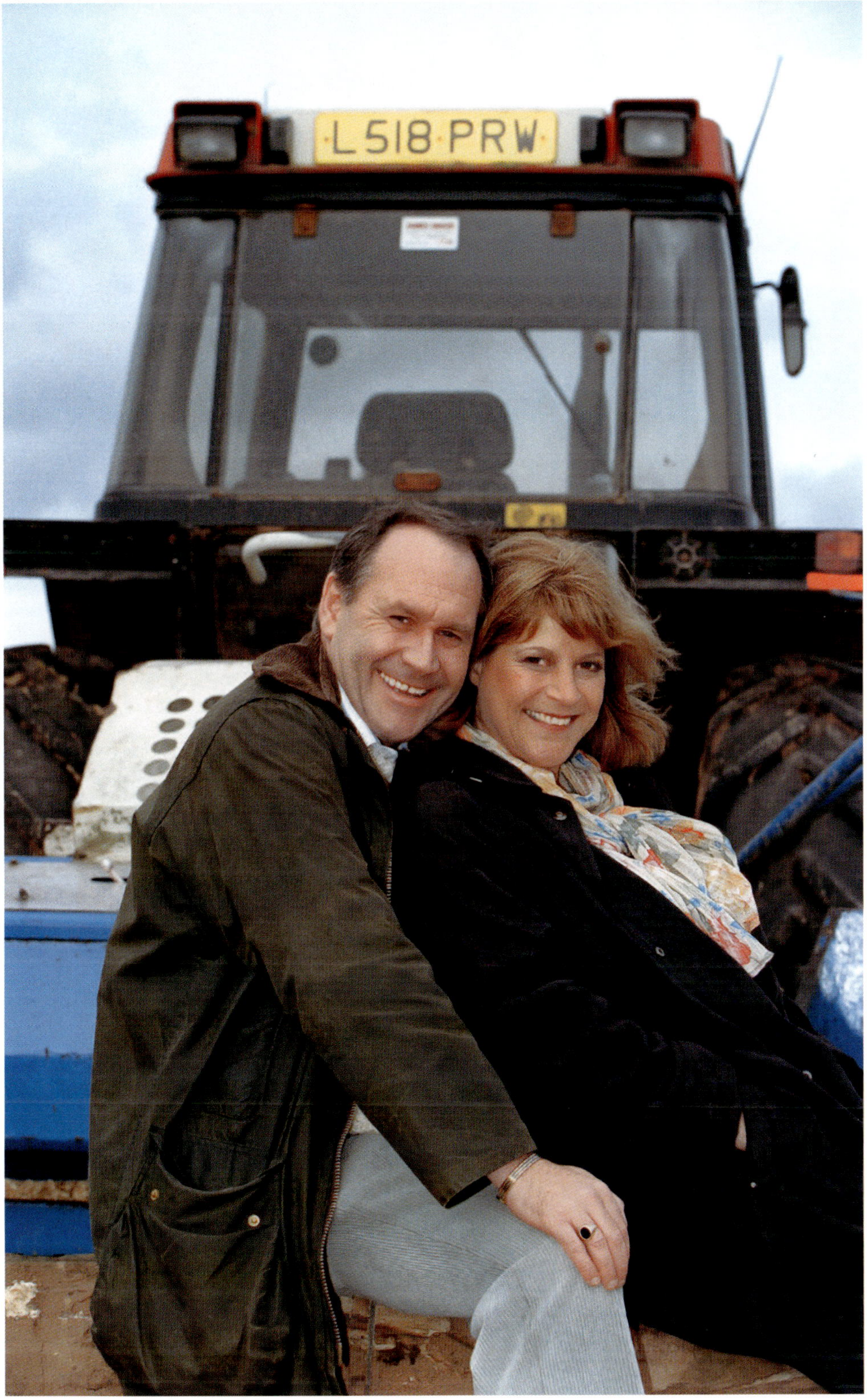
L518 PRW

MARCH

WEEK 12
2009

16 Monday

17 Tuesday

St. Patrick's Day
Holiday, Northern Ireland and Republic of Ireland

18 Wednesday

Last Quarter
NEWS OF NELSON GABRIEL'S DEATH 2001

19 Thursday

20 Friday

Vernal Equinox

21 Saturday

22 Sunday

Mothering Sunday, UK

MARCH

WEEK 13
2009

23 Monday

24 Tuesday

25 Wednesday

26 Thursday *New Moon*

27 Friday

28 Saturday

29 Sunday British Summer Time begins

AMBRIDGE LANDMARKS
Lower Loxley Hall

THE DETAILS:

Location: North East of Ambridge
Age: Built in 1702 by the Pargetter family, grade II listed
Style: Jacobean with later additions
Facilities: 70 acres of parkland including: conference centre, wedding reception hall, visitor access, art gallery, treetop walk, rare breeds petting area, falconry, shop, café, cycle trails, wild flower meadow
Owners: Nigel and Elizabeth Pargetter
Resident: Lewis Carmichael, step-father to Nigel
Staff: Includes Head Gardener: Mr. Titcombe; Housekeeper: Mrs. Titcombe (formerly Pugsley); Gushing Guide: Bert Fry; Shop and Café Manager: Kathy Perks

TO THE MANOR BORN:

The pinnacle of the Lower Loxley Estate, Lower Loxley Hall is a grand mansion that sits in three acres of formal gardens and nearly 400 acres of ancient parkland. Nigel Pargetter inherited the property in March 1988 after the death of his father. He endeavours to maintain the house and grounds, overcoming the property-perils of dry rot and death-watch beetle, and continues to live in the manner to which he is accustomed. In 1996, Nigel and Elizabeth agreed to open the house to visitors in an attempt to raise money to preserve their crumbling home. With this extra income, they have improved the property offering entertainments for all the family, business amenities, and eco-friendly wedding facilities. Nigel also launched Lower Loxley wine in 2006.

Elizabeth endeavours to keep up with Nigel's crazes, reining him in on occasion as co-manager of Lower Loxley, while keeping an eye on their two children.

IF WALLS HAD EARS...

- ...they'd ache with the past complaints of Nigel's interfering mother, Julia. They'd also have been shocked to hear the scandalous home truths revealed by her sister, Ellen. Julia's real name was Joan and, far from moneyed, 'Julia' was in fact the daughter of a greengrocer.

- ...they would ring with myriad sounds from engines to battle cries as a result of the various events held at the Hall including a transport festival, Sealed Knot re-enactment and mysterious murder weekend.

- ...they'd cover them when Elizabeth 'helped' the police with their enquiries into the rape of Kathy Perks by ex Lower Loxley chef, Owen King (alias Gareth Taylor)

SOUNDBITE:
The beautiful grounds of Lower Loxley Hall just wouldn't be the same without the proud strut and striking call of the peacocks who decorate its lawns. There are so many peacocks at Lower Loxley that different calls from many birds are taken from the BBC sound effects library.

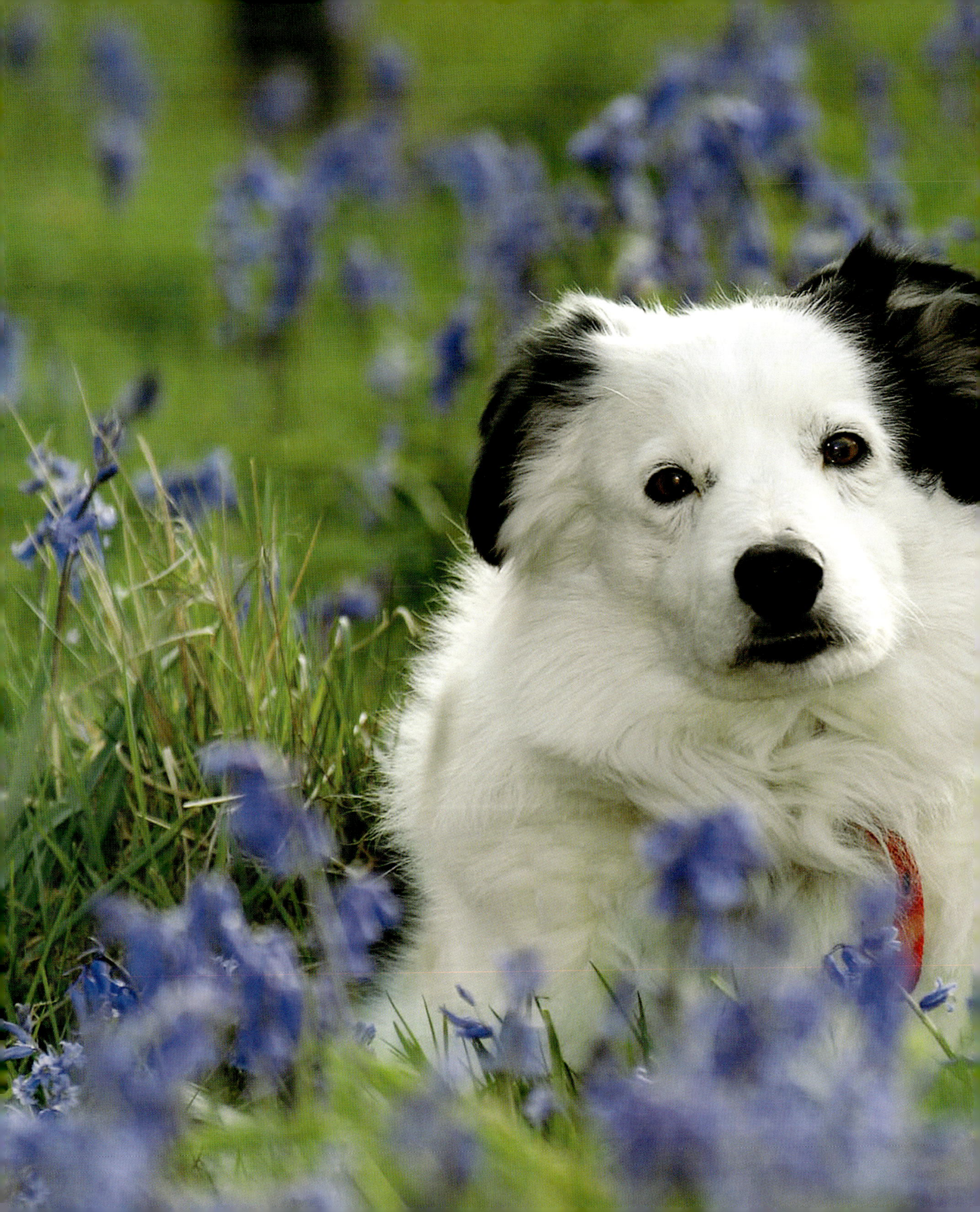

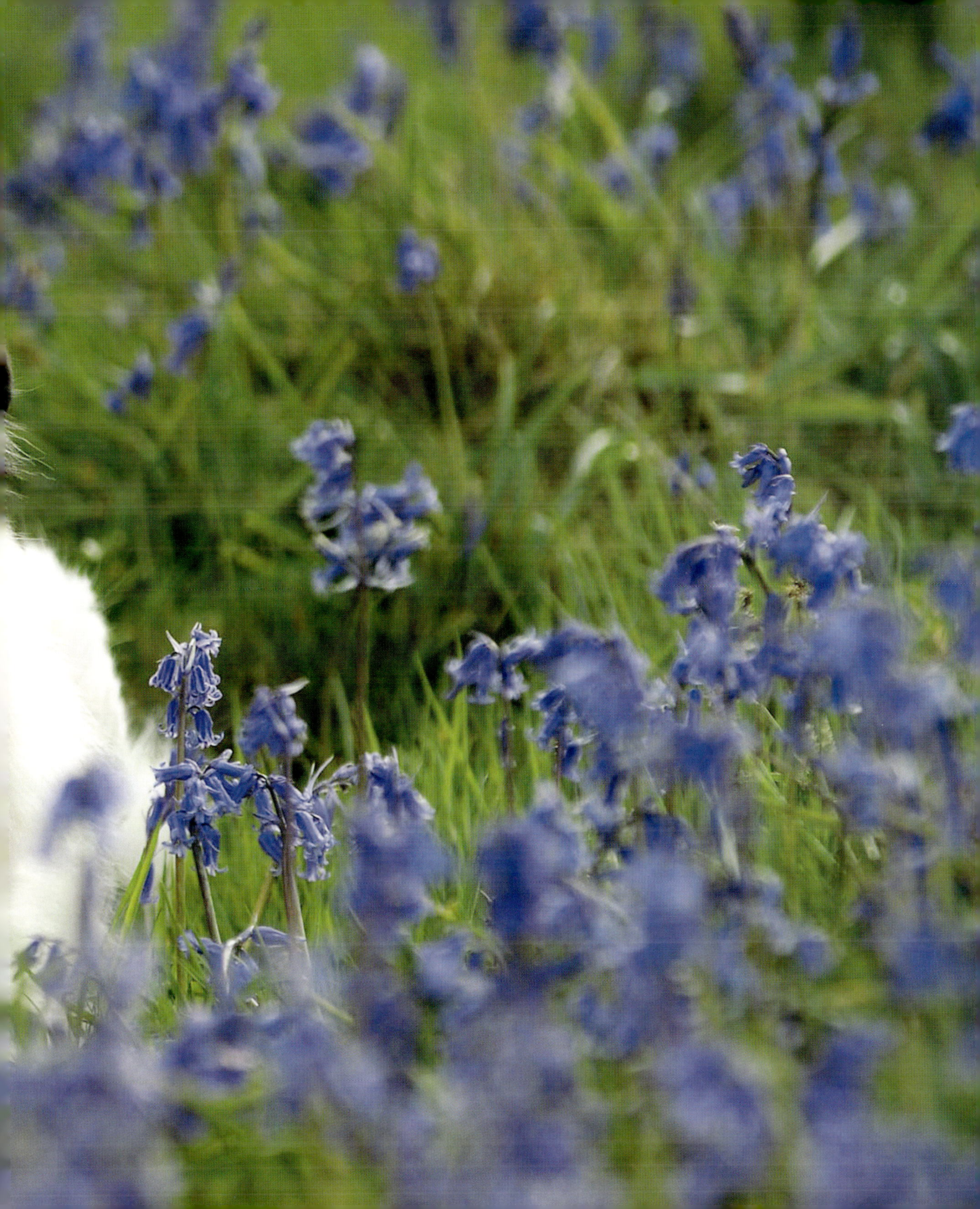

MARCH | APRIL

WEEK 14
2009

30 Monday
JAMES BELLAMY BORN 1973

31 Tuesday

1 Wednesday

2 Thursday
First Quarter
GRACE ARCHER BORN 1929

3 Friday
CAROLINE STERLING BORN 1955

4 Saturday

5 Sunday
Palm Sunday
ROBERT SNELL BORN 1943

APRIL

WEEK 15
2009

6 Monday

7 Tuesday

GEORGE GRUNDY BORN 2005

8 Wednesday

9 Thursday

Full Moon
Maundy Thursday
Passover (Pesach), First Day

10 Friday

Good Friday
Holiday, UK, Canada, USA,
Australia and New Zealand

11 Saturday

PHIL AND GRACE ARCHER MARRIED 1955

12 Sunday

Easter Day
GUY PEMBERTON DIED 1996
KATE AND LUCAS MADIKANE MARRIED 2001
FIRST SUNDAY EPISODE 1998

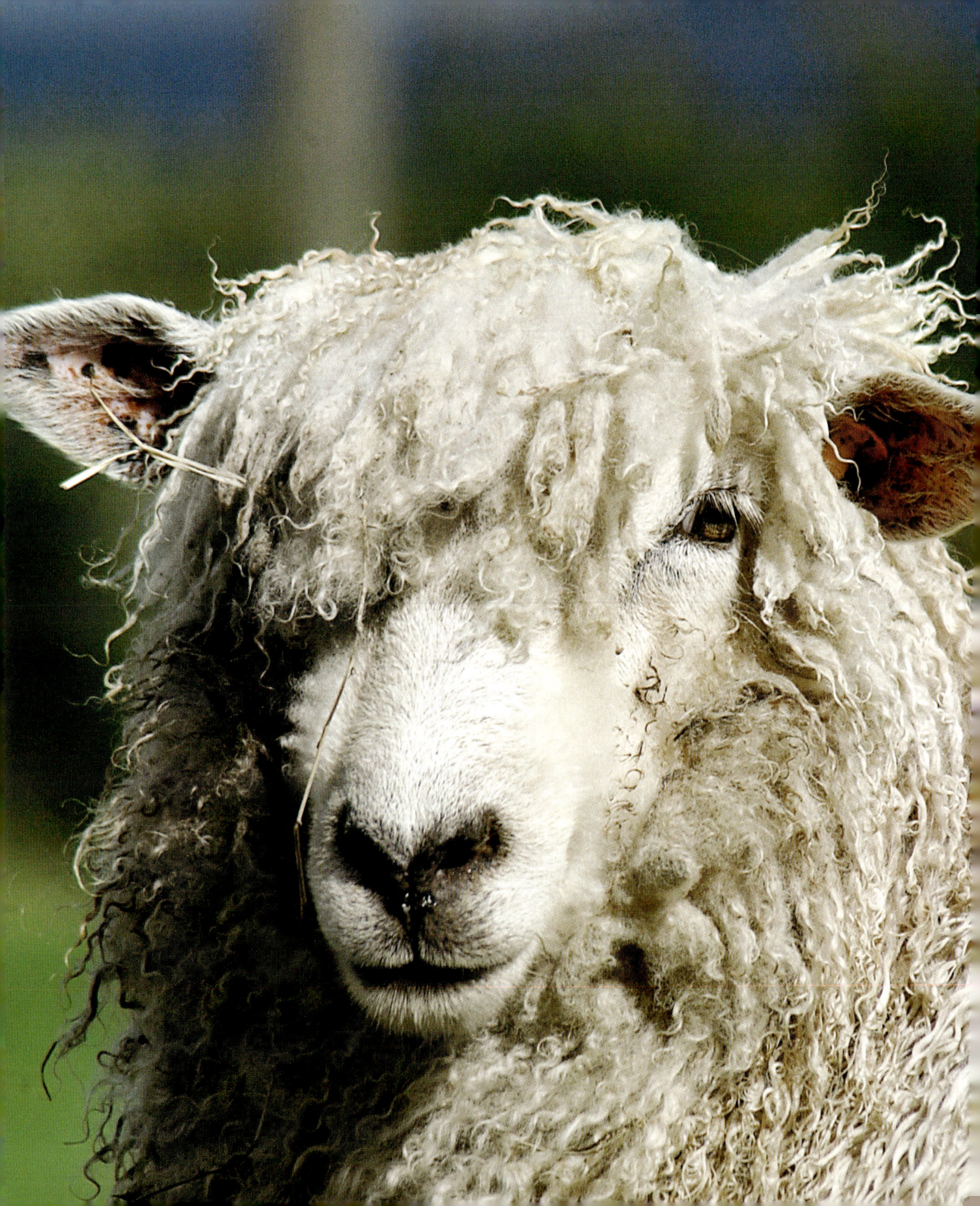

APRIL

WEEK 16
2009

13 Monday

Easter Monday
Holiday, UK (exc. Scotland), Republic of Ireland, Canada, Australia and New Zealand

14 Tuesday

15 Wednesday

Passover (Pesach), Seventh Day

16 Thursday

Passover (Pesach), Eighth Day
HELEN ARCHER BORN 1979

17 Friday

Last Quarter

18 Saturday

19 Sunday

OMNIBUS LENGTHENED TO 1HR 15 MINS 1998

APRIL

WEEK 17
2009

20 Monday

21 Tuesday

Birthday of Queen Elizabeth II
ELIZABETH PARGETTER BORN 1967

22 Wednesday

23 Thursday

St. George's Day
PHIL ARCHER BORN 1928
DAN ARCHER DIED 1986

24 Friday

KATHY AND SID PERKS MARRIED 1987

25 Saturday

Holiday, Australia and New Zealand (Anzac Day)
New Moon

26 Sunday

KENTON ARCHER (RICHARD ATTLEE) AND KATHY PERKS (HEDLI NIKLAUS)

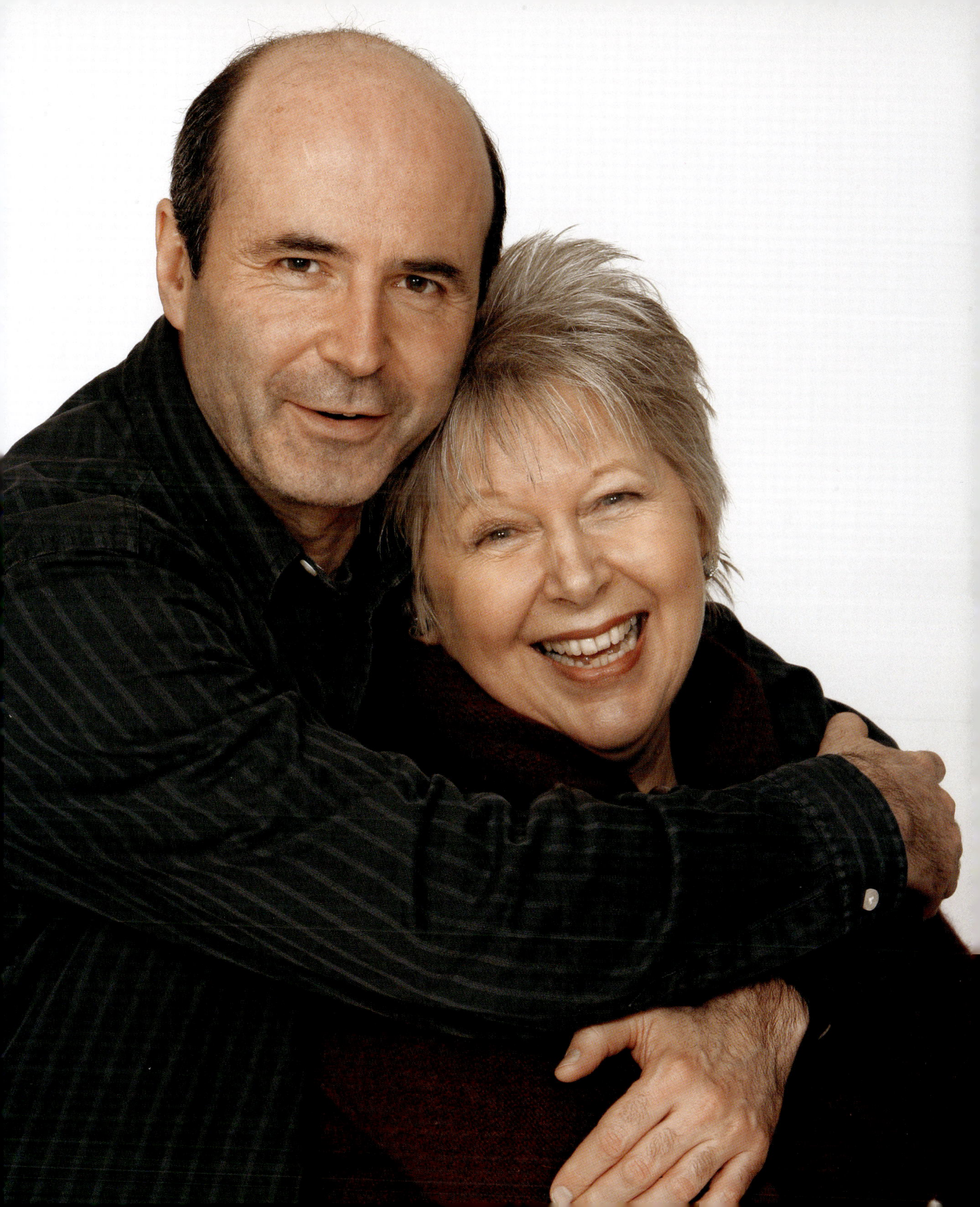

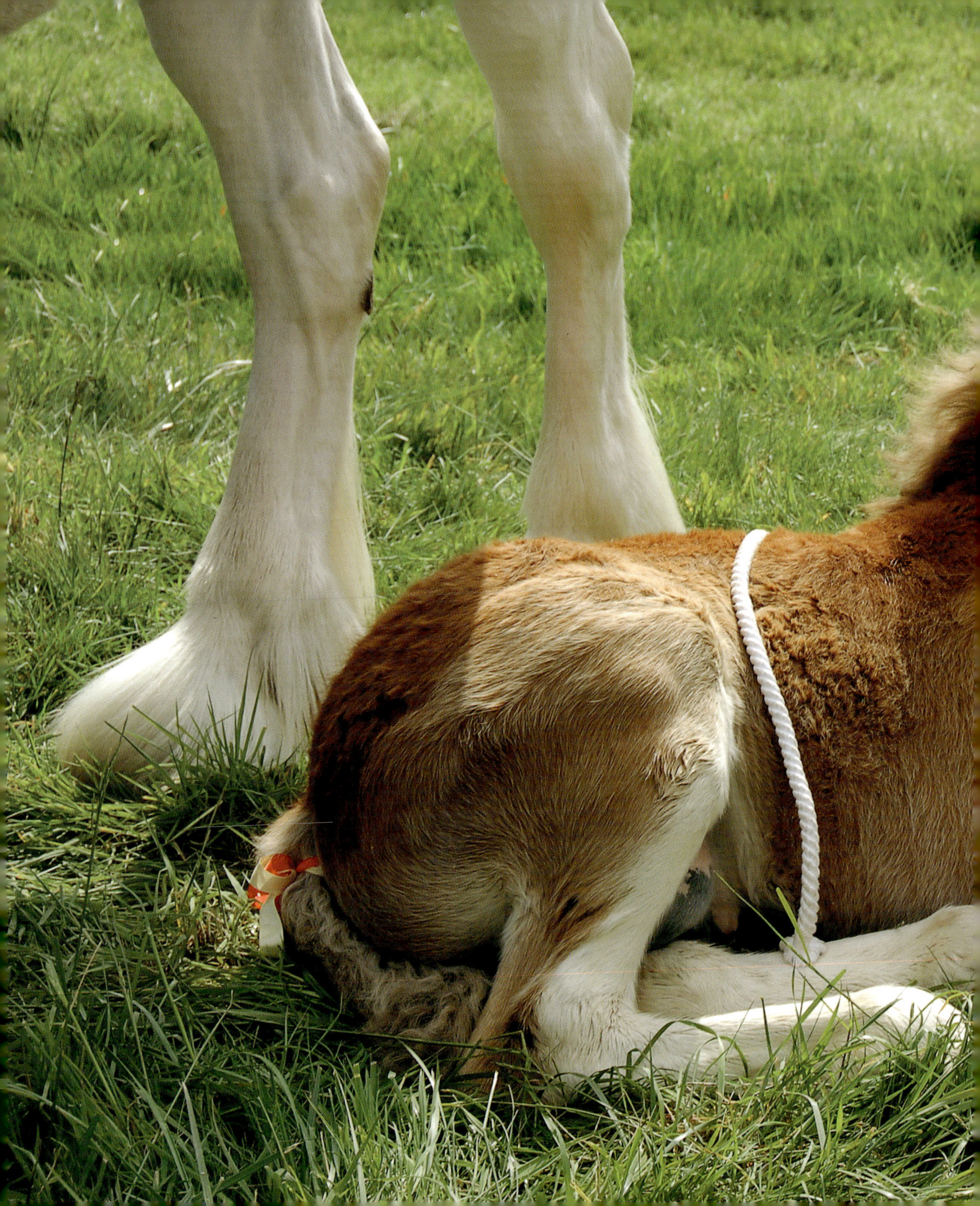

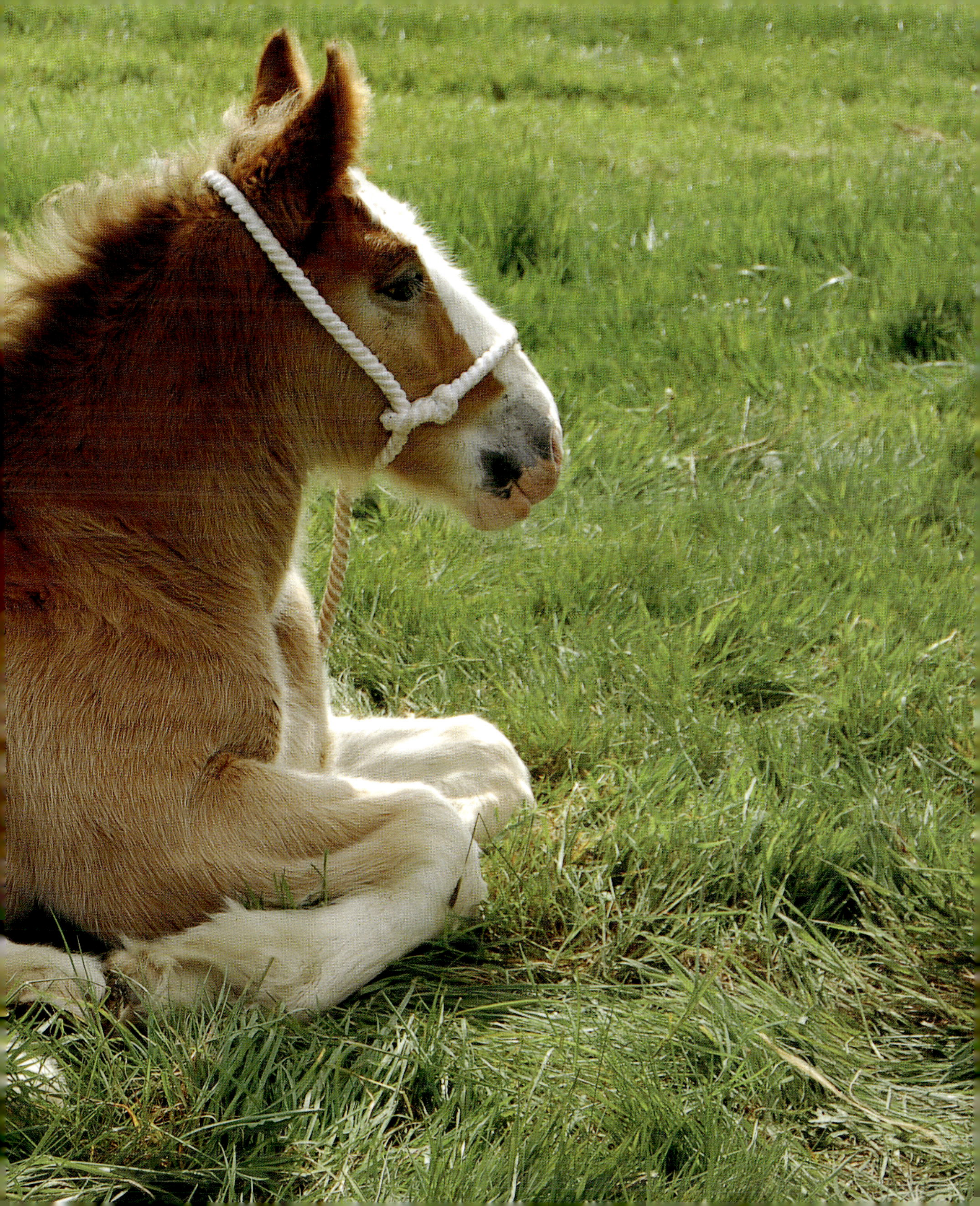

APRIL | MAY

WEEK 18
2009

27 Monday

28 Tuesday

29 Wednesday

30 Thursday

1 Friday

First Quarter
HAYLEY TUCKER BORN 1977

2 Saturday

3 Sunday

MAY

WEEK 19
2009

4 Monday — Early Spring Bank Holiday, UK and Republic of Ireland

5 Tuesday

6 Wednesday

7 Thursday — HAYLEY AND ROY TUCKER MARRIED 2001
GREG TURNER DIED 2004

8 Friday

9 Saturday — *Full Moon*

10 Sunday — Mother's Day, USA, Canada, Australia and New Zealand

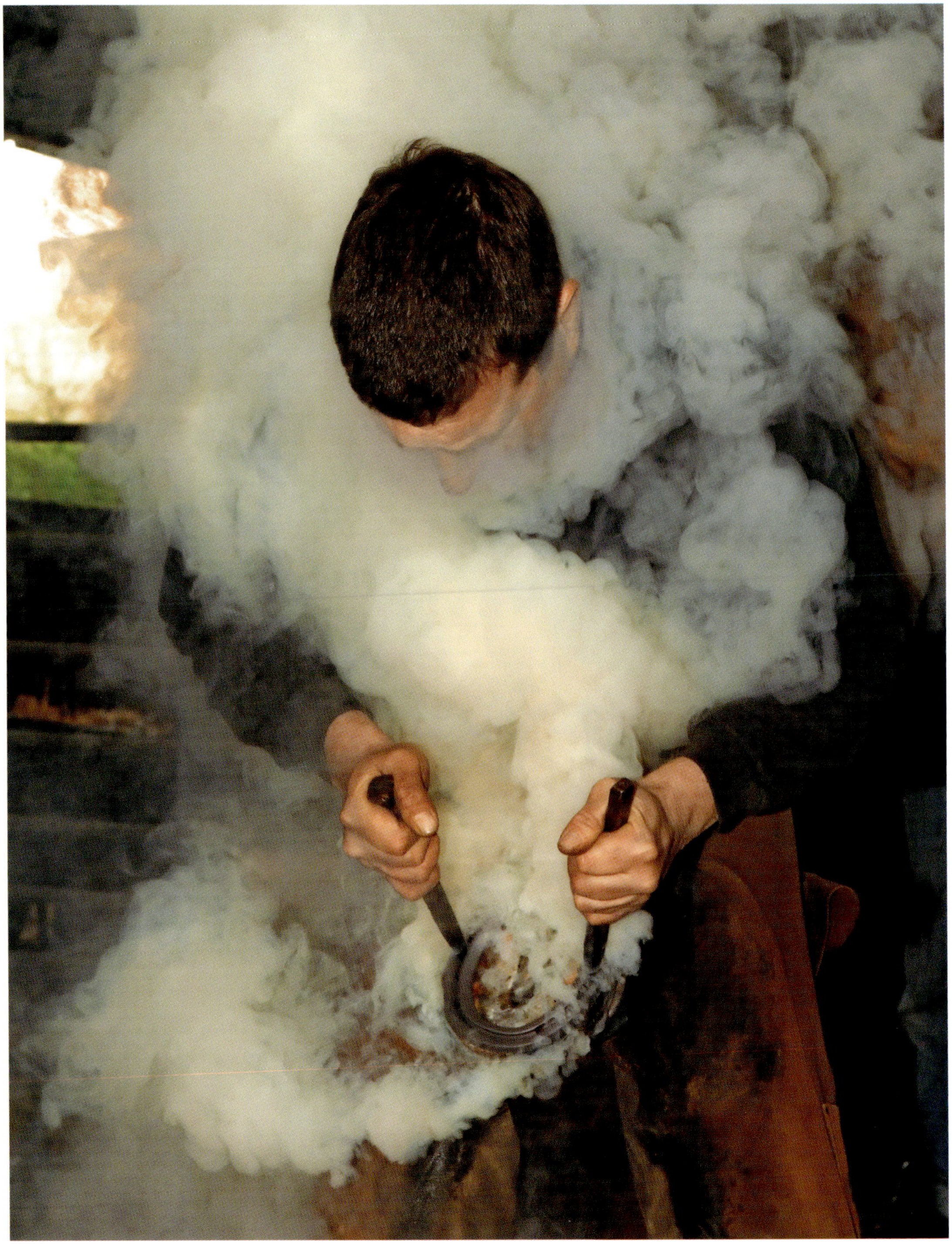

MAY

WEEK 20
2009

| 11 | Monday | MERIEL ARCHER BORN 2001 |

| 12 | Tuesday | DEBBIE AND SIMON GERRARD MARRIED 2000
CLARRIE GRUNDY BORN 1954 |

| 13 | Wednesday | |

| 14 | Thursday | **FIVE TRIAL EPISODES RECORDED 1950** |

| 15 | Friday | |

| 16 | Saturday | |

| 17 | Sunday | *Last Quarter* |

MAY

WEEK 21
2009

18 Monday — Holiday, Canada (Victoria Day)

19 Tuesday

20 Wednesday

21 Thursday — Ascension Day

22 Friday — NEIL CARTER BORN 1957

23 Saturday

24 Sunday — *New Moon*

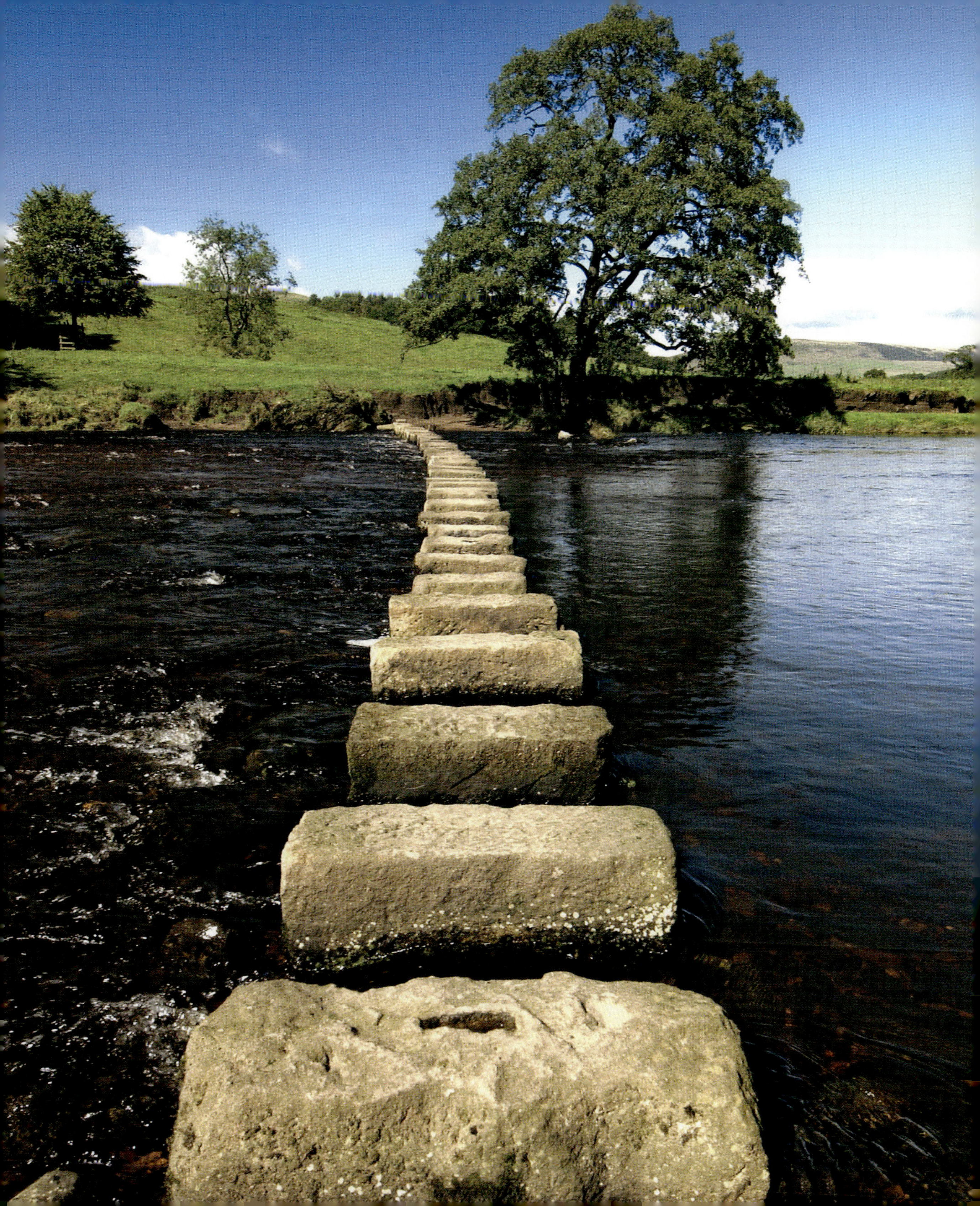

LOWER LOXLEY HALL

NAUGHTY NIBBLES!
ELIZABETH'S ASPARAGUS APPETISER

There's nothing that the team at Lower Loxley doesn't know about catering, so get your party off with a swing and impress your colleagues with this lovely little Lower Loxley appetiser. It's a wonderful mix of sweet and salty flavours and a real winner with drinks before dinner.

Serves 12

INGREDIENTS

3 bunches of thin asparagus
12 slices of prosciutto or Parma ham
200ml (7oz) quality balsamic vinegar

METHOD

- Pour the balsamic vinegar into a small saucepan and place over a low heat until it has been reduced by two-thirds, then remove and allow to cool.
- Trim the woody bases off the asparagus and cut each spear into three sections.
- Blanch the asparagus pieces until vibrant and green (less than 1 minute), then strain and plunge into iced water and allow to cool.
- Cut the slices of prosciutto lengthwise to form long ribbons about an inch thick.
- Arrange two stem pieces and one tip piece of asparagus and bind with a piece of prosciutto. Repeat.
- Arrange asparagus bundles on a serving platter and drizzle some of the reduced balsamic on each immediately before serving.

☆ NIGEL'S TOP TIP ☆

"To make a truly distinctive impression, serve with a fine glass of Lower Loxley wine."

MAY

WEEK 22
2009

25 Monday

Spring Bank Holiday, UK
Holiday, USA (Memorial Day)

26 Tuesday

JULIA AND LEWIS CARMICHAEL MARRIED 2005

27 Wednesday

28 Thursday

29 Friday

Feast of Weeks (Shavuot)
JENNIFER AND BRIAN ALDRIDGE MARRIED 1976
LYNDA SNELL BORN 1947
***THE ARCHERS* FIRST BROADCAST IN MIDLAND REGION 1950**

30 Saturday

31 Sunday

Whit Sunday (Pentecost)
First Quarter
SIOBHAN HATHAWAY DIED 2007

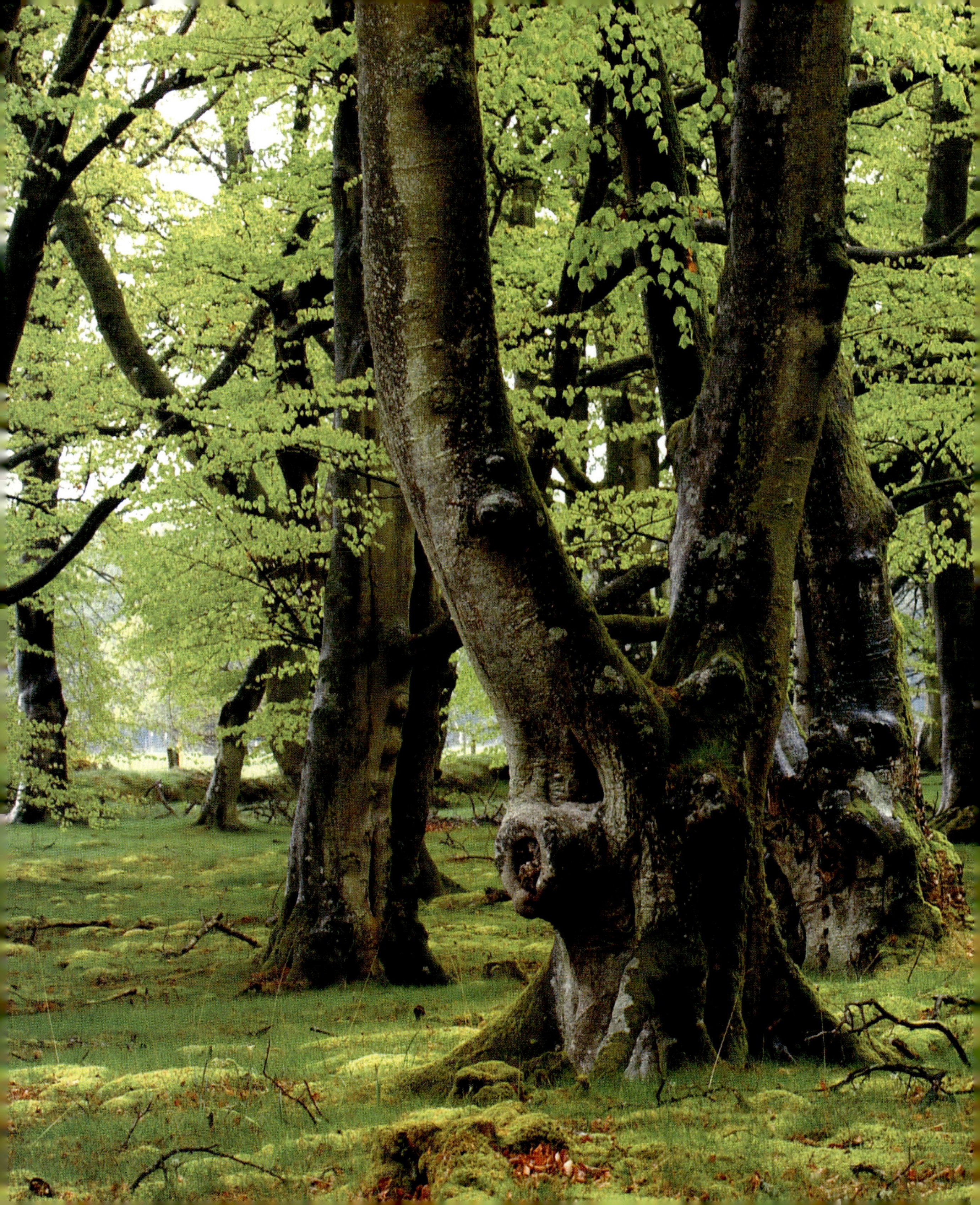

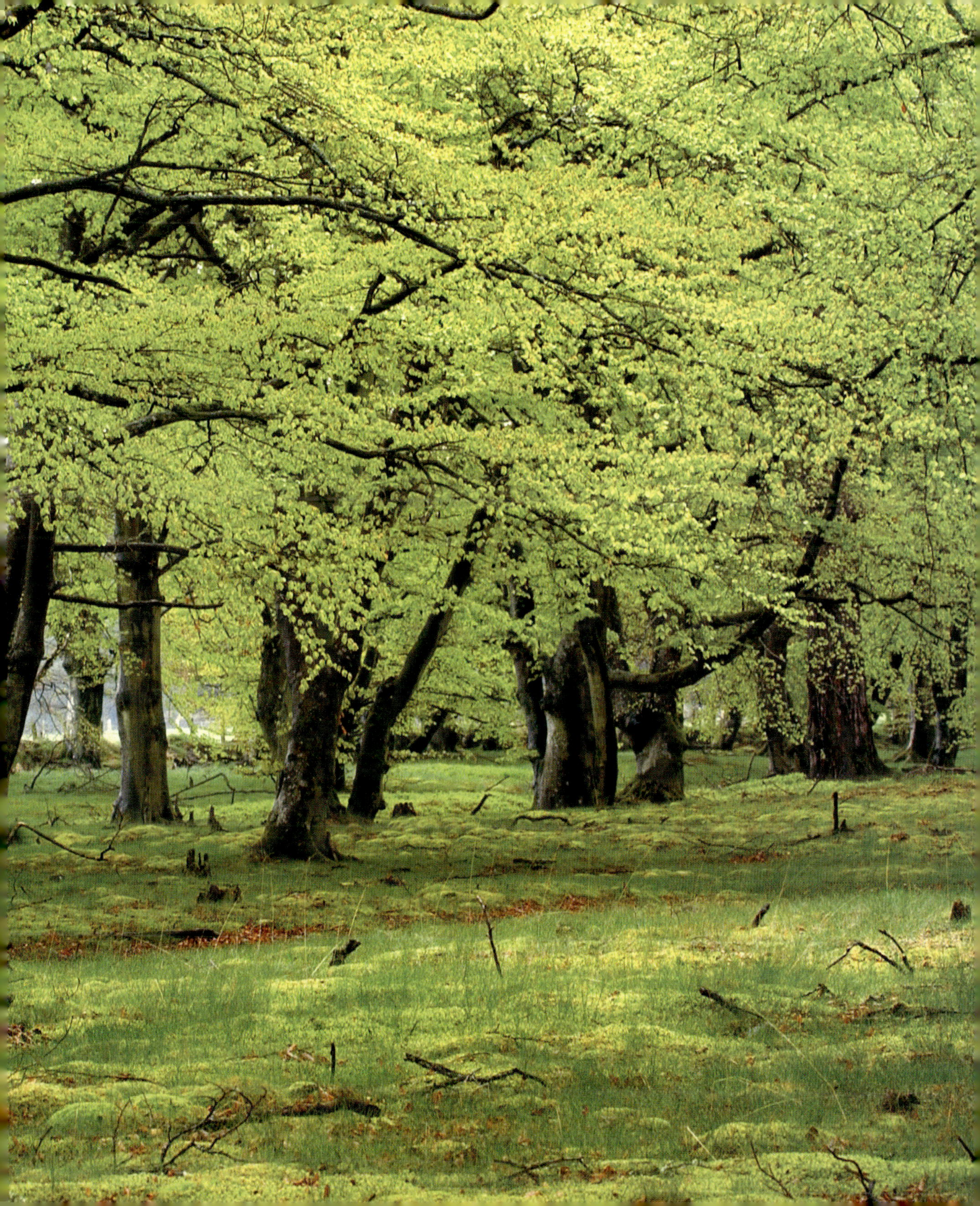

JUNE

WEEK 23
2009

1 Monday
Holiday, Republic of Ireland
Holiday, New Zealand (Queen's Birthday)

2 Tuesday
Coronation Day

3 Wednesday

4 Thursday

5 Friday

6 Saturday

7 Sunday
Trinity Sunday
Full Moon

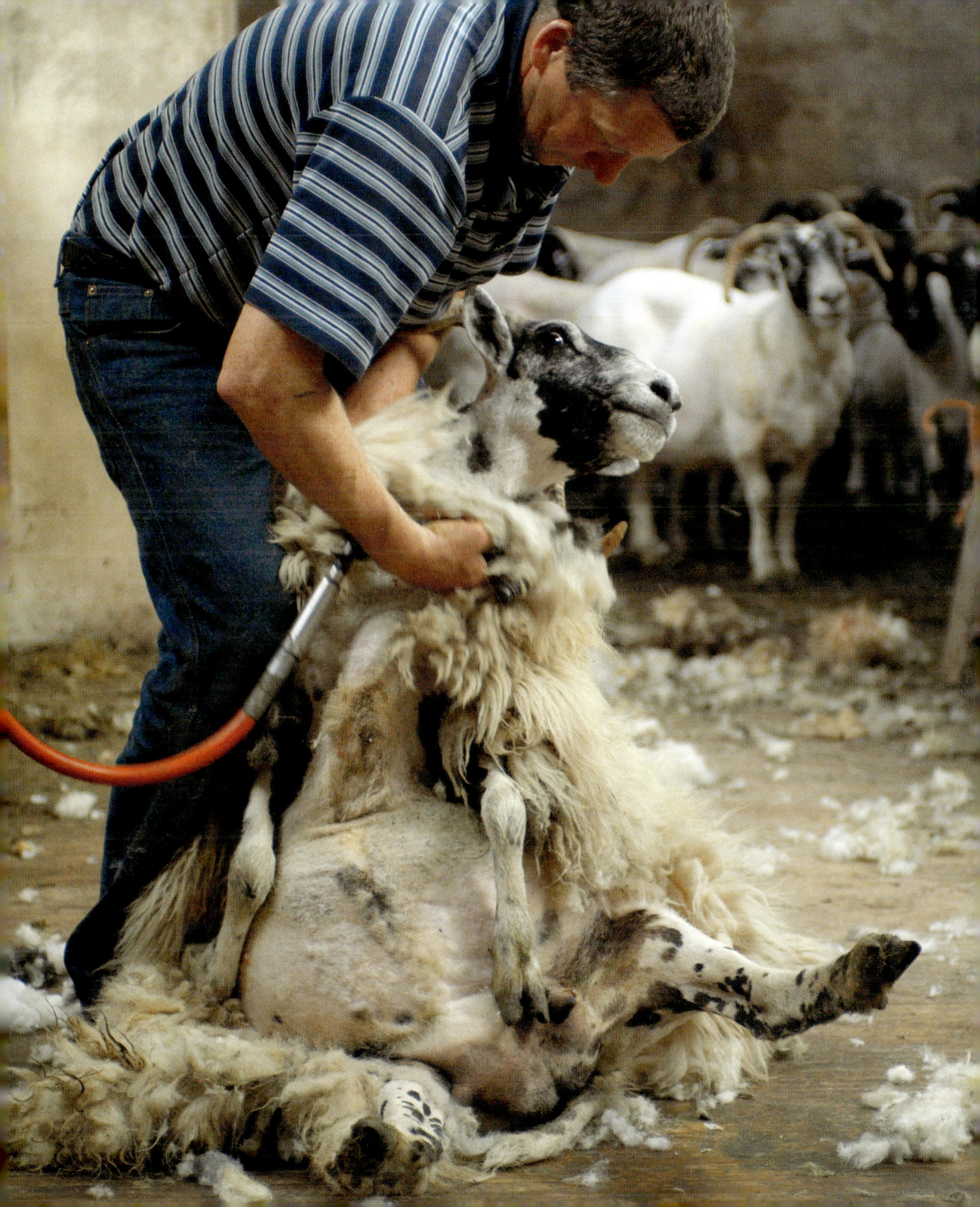

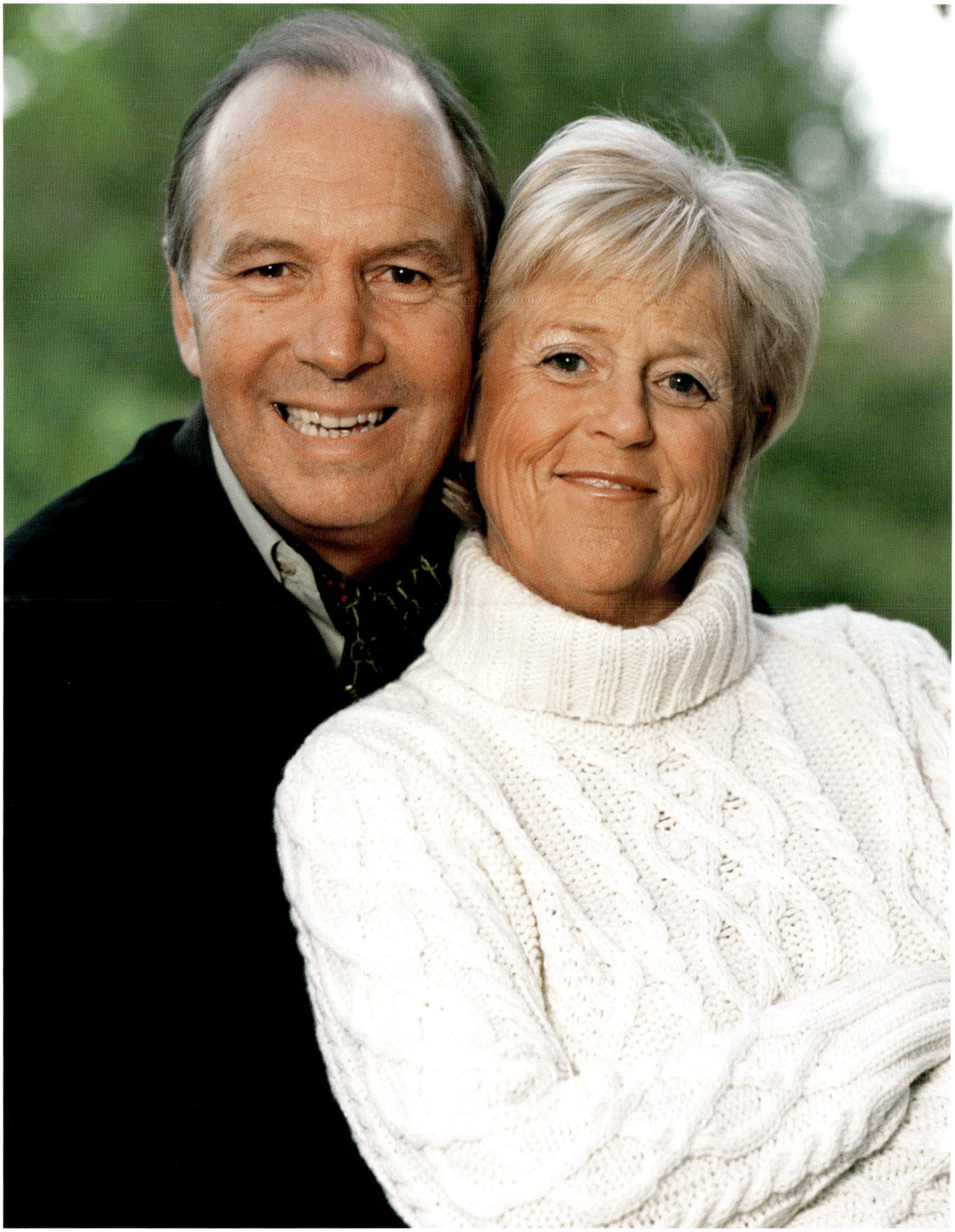

JUNE

WEEK 24
2009

8 Monday

NIGEL PARGETTER BORN 1959
***THE ARCHERS* FIRST BROADCAST IN STEREO 1992**

9 Tuesday

SID PERKS BORN 1944

10 Wednesday

11 Thursday

Corpus Christi

12 Friday

13 Saturday

The Queen's Official Birthday
SIOBHAN HATHAWAY BORN 1965

14 Sunday

JENNIFER AND BRIAN ALDRIDGE (ANGELA PIPER AND CHARLES COLLINGWOOD)

JUNE

WEEK 25
2009

15 Monday

St. Swithin's Day
Last Quarter

16 Tuesday

RUTH ARCHER BORN 1968

17 Wednesday

USHA GUPTA BORN 1962

18 Thursday

19 Friday

FALLON ROGERS BORN 1985

20 Saturday

21 Sunday

Summer Solstice
Father's Day, UK, Canada and USA

JUNE

WEEK 26
2009

22 Monday

New Moon
ADAM MACY BORN 1967
CHRISTOPHER CARTER BORN 1988

23 Tuesday

24 Wednesday

25 Thursday

26 Friday

27 Saturday

28 Sunday

PHOEBE ALDRIDGE BORN 1998

AMBRIDGE LANDMARKS
Grey Gables

THE DETAILS:

Location: West of the village of Ambridge
Age: Built in the Victorian era, Grey Gables was designed by Benjamin Perry in 1898, and last modernised in 2004.
Style: Faux Gothic
Facilities: 60 bedrooms (all en-suite), restaurant, bars, ballroom, health club with swimming pool, several function rooms and gardens.
Owners: Caroline and Oliver Sterling
Staff: Includes Manager: Caroline Sterling; Deputy Manager: Roy Tucker; Chef: Ian Craig; Senior Receptionist: Lynda Snell.
Awards: 1984 – Grey Gables restaurant won the Golden Rosette gourmet award.

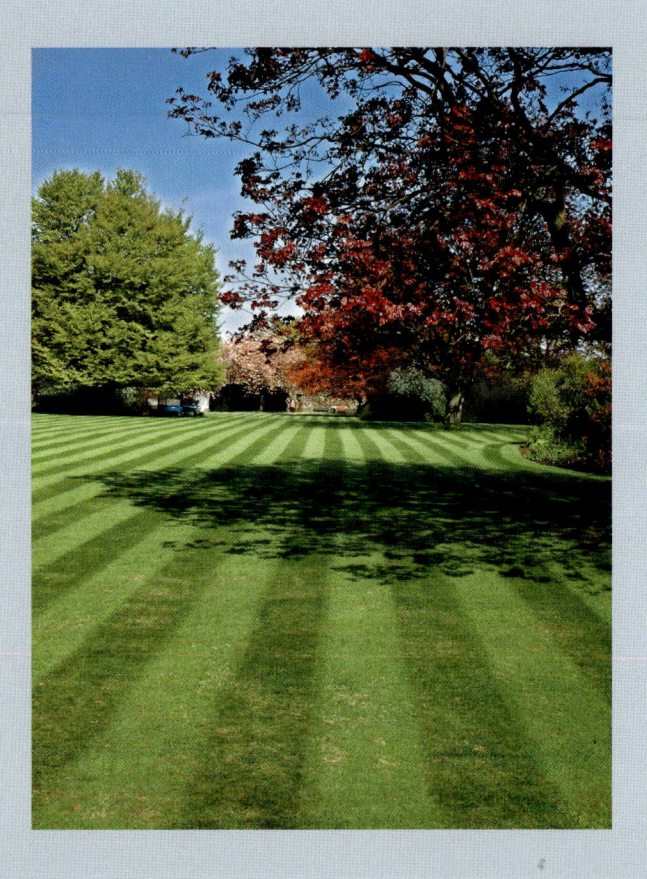

GOTHIC GABLES AND GRAND EVENTS:

In 1958, Reggie and Valerie Trentham sold Grey Gables Country Club to Jack Woolley and left Ambridge. Already a well-established business man, Jack bought twenty acres of land from local entrepreneur Charles Grenville to turn into a golf course, and began building the opulent Grey Gables empire. The property underwent a grand refurbishment in 2004 but sadly, in the following year, Jack developed Alzheimer's and was forced to put Grey Gables on the market. This tough decision was welcomed by hotel manager, Caroline Pemberton. Together with future husband Oliver Sterling she pulled out all the stops to put in a successful bid and was overjoyed when Grey Gables became hers in 2006. Caroline continues to run the hotel ably assisted by deputy manager Roy Tucker, chef Ian Craig and senior receptionist Lynda Snell.

IF WALLS HAD EARS...

- ...they would have heard some right royal gossip when HRH Princess Margaret and the Duke of Westminster stayed at Grey Gables in 1984 for the Borsetshire NSPCC centenary fashion show. The regal legacy lives on to this day as one of the rooms was named 'The Royal Garden Suite' in honour of the Princess.

- ...they would echo with the sounds of Grace Archer's screams as she screamed "Fire!" on 22nd September, 1955. Phil had arranged a meal at Grey Gables with Carol Grey and John Tregorran. Grace went outside to search for a lost earring only to discover the stables were on fire. She plunged into the blaze to save Christine's horse Midnight but her brave effort ended in tragedy and she was trapped under a fallen beam. Midnight survived, but Grace lost her life in one of the most dramatic events ever to happen in *The Archers*. Right: Christine Johnson (Lesley Saweard) with Midnight.

- ...they would be as confused as Roy Tucker by the hissing sound coming from a cupboard in Grey Gables. Bertie the boa constrictor had found a new home! (To everyone's great surprise, he later rejected Grey Gables and was found curled up in Lynda's bed!) But it was his owner, Scarlett del Monte who caused the *real* stir among the lusty men and jealous women of Ambridge...

SOUNDBITE:
Many weddings and anniversaries have been celebrated at Grey Gables, most recently that of Caroline and Oliver Sterling (Sara Coward and Michael Cochrane), see right, and champagne corks are frequently a-popping. Inventive sound artists in The Archers studio use a trusty bicycle pump with a cork on the end – it's cheaper than Brut and the actors can still read their scripts!

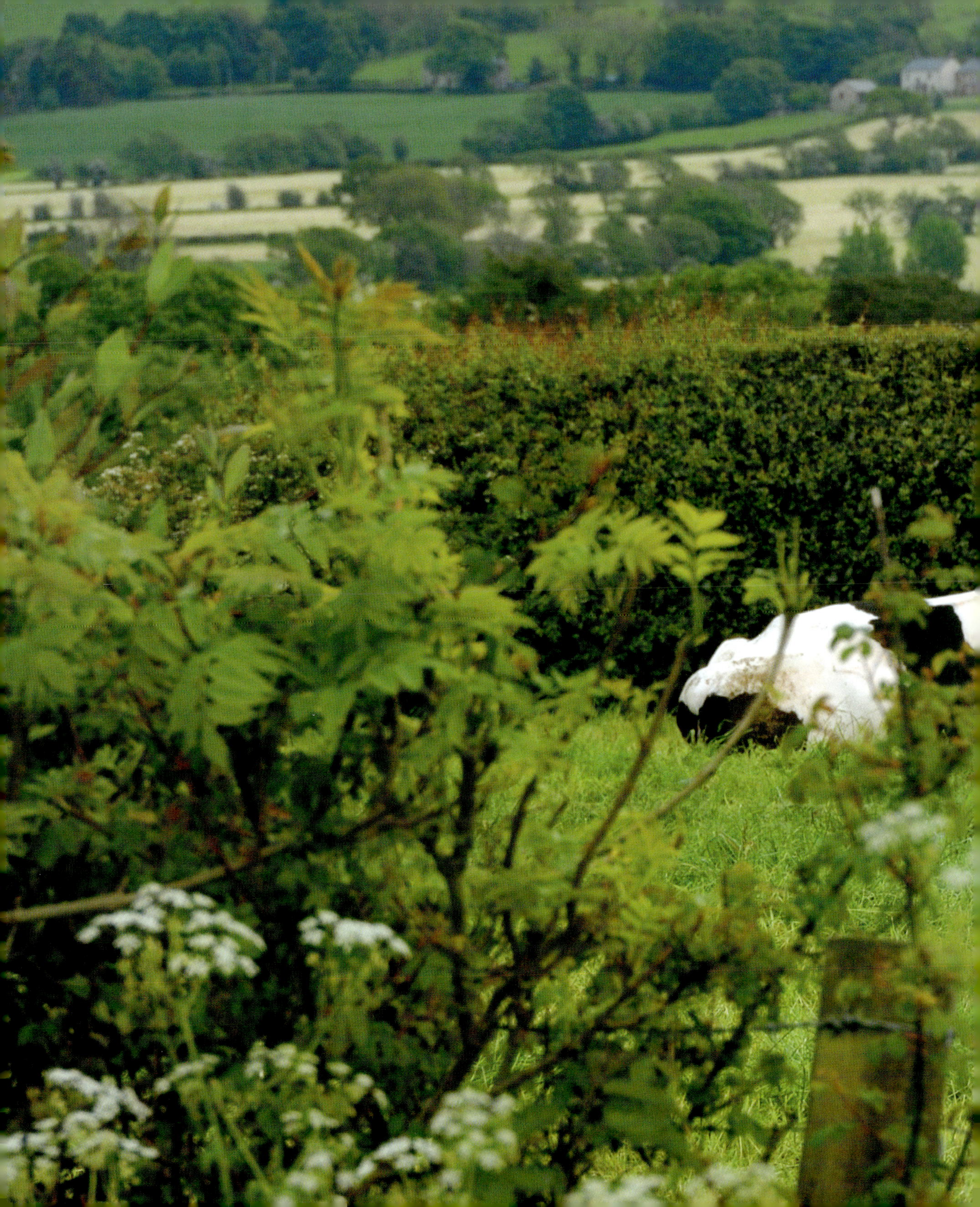

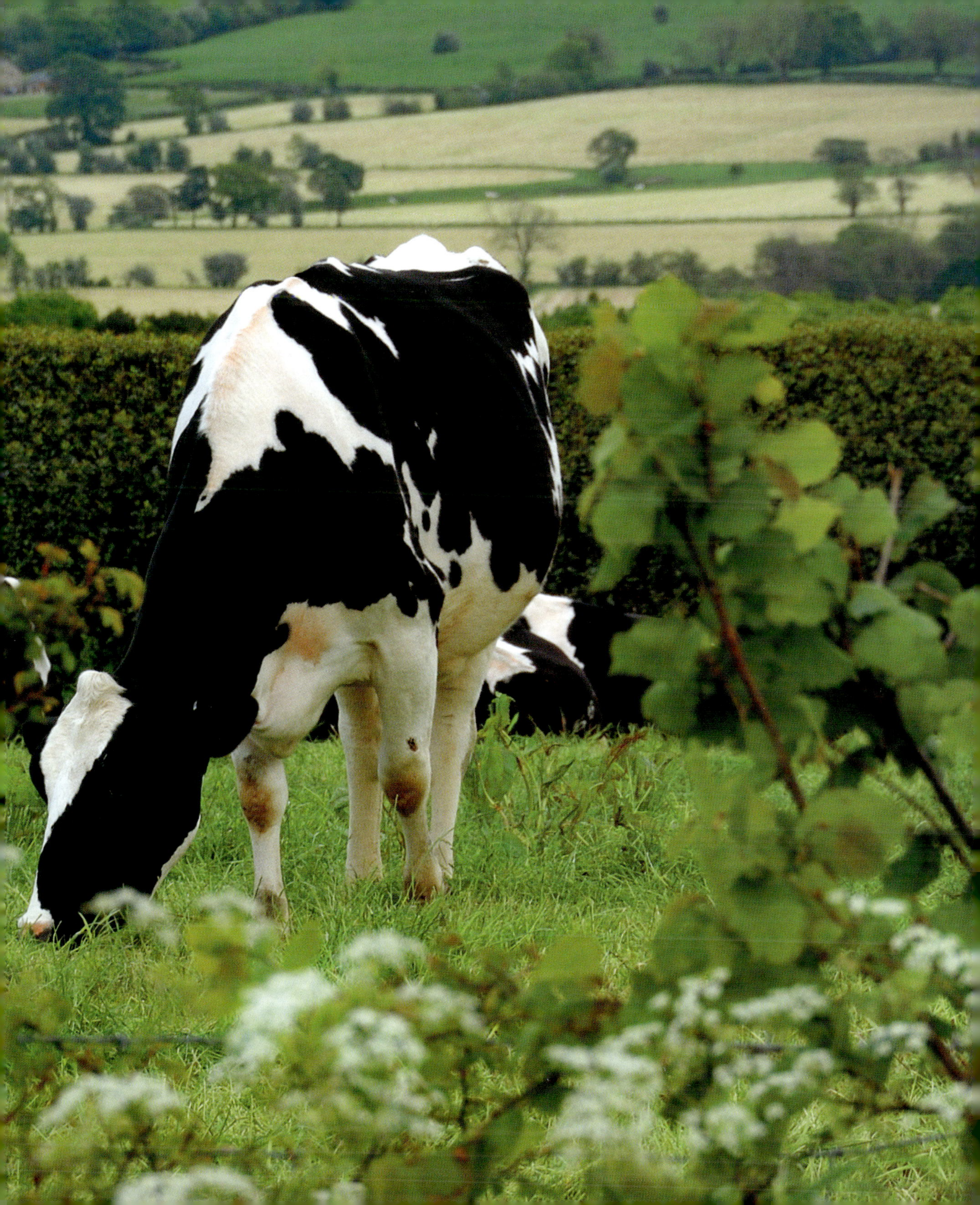

JUNE | JULY

WEEK 27
2009

29 Monday

First Quarter
CAROLINE AND OLIVER STERLING MARRIED 2006

30 Tuesday

1 Wednesday

Holiday, Canada (Canada Day)

2 Thursday

3 Friday

Holiday, USA (Independence Day)

4 Saturday

Independence Day, USA
JOLENE AND SID PERKS MARRIED 2002

5 Sunday

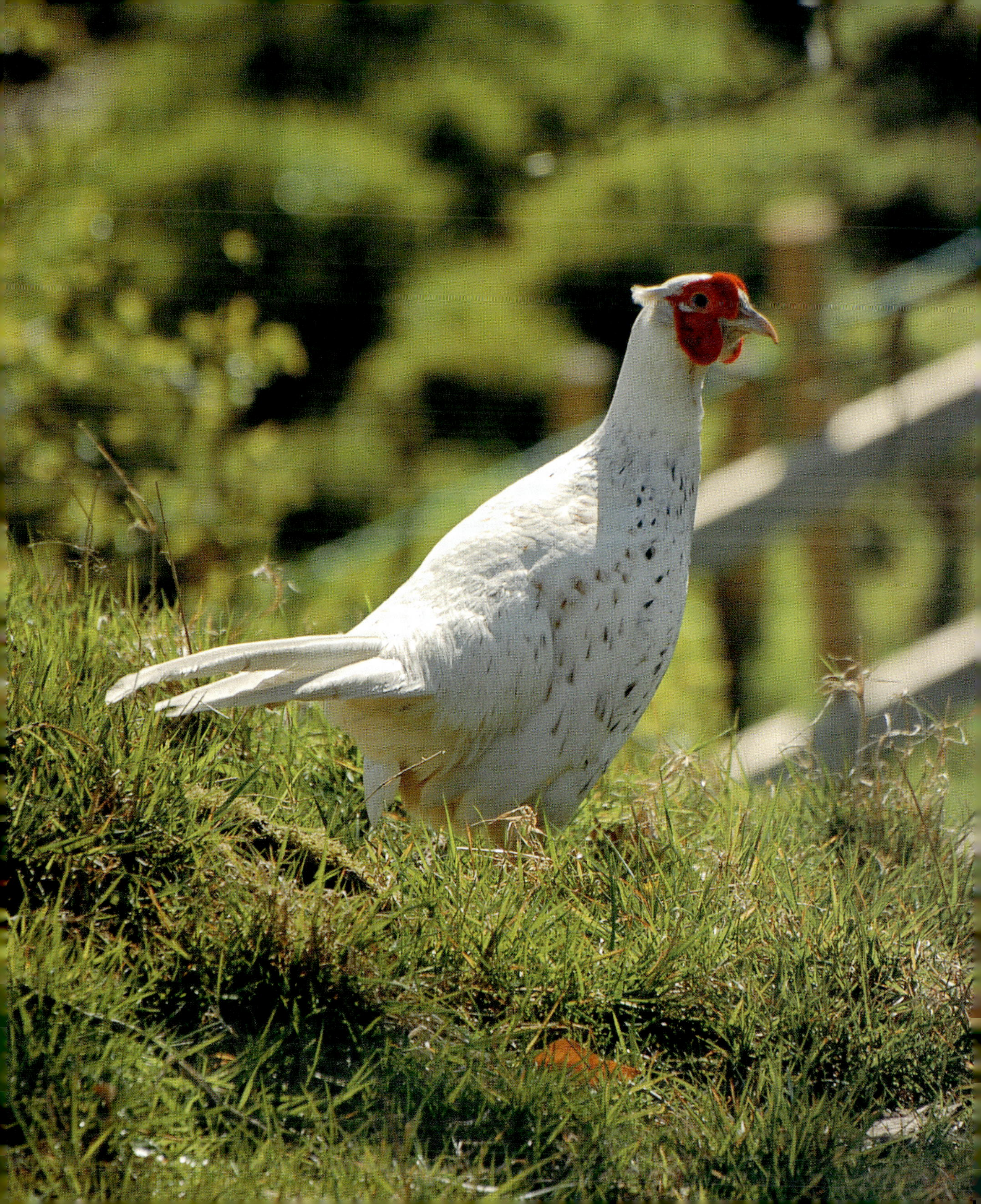

JULY

WEEK 28
2009

6 Monday

7 Tuesday   *Full Moon*

8 Wednesday   LILIAN BELLAMY BORN 1947

9 Thursday

10 Friday

11 Saturday   DORIS ARCHER BORN 1900

12 Sunday

JULY

WEEK 29
2009

13 Monday

Battle of the Boyne
Holiday, Northern Ireland

14 Tuesday

15 Wednesday

Last Quarter

16 Thursday

17 Friday

18 Saturday

19 Sunday

JACK WOOLLEY BORN 1919

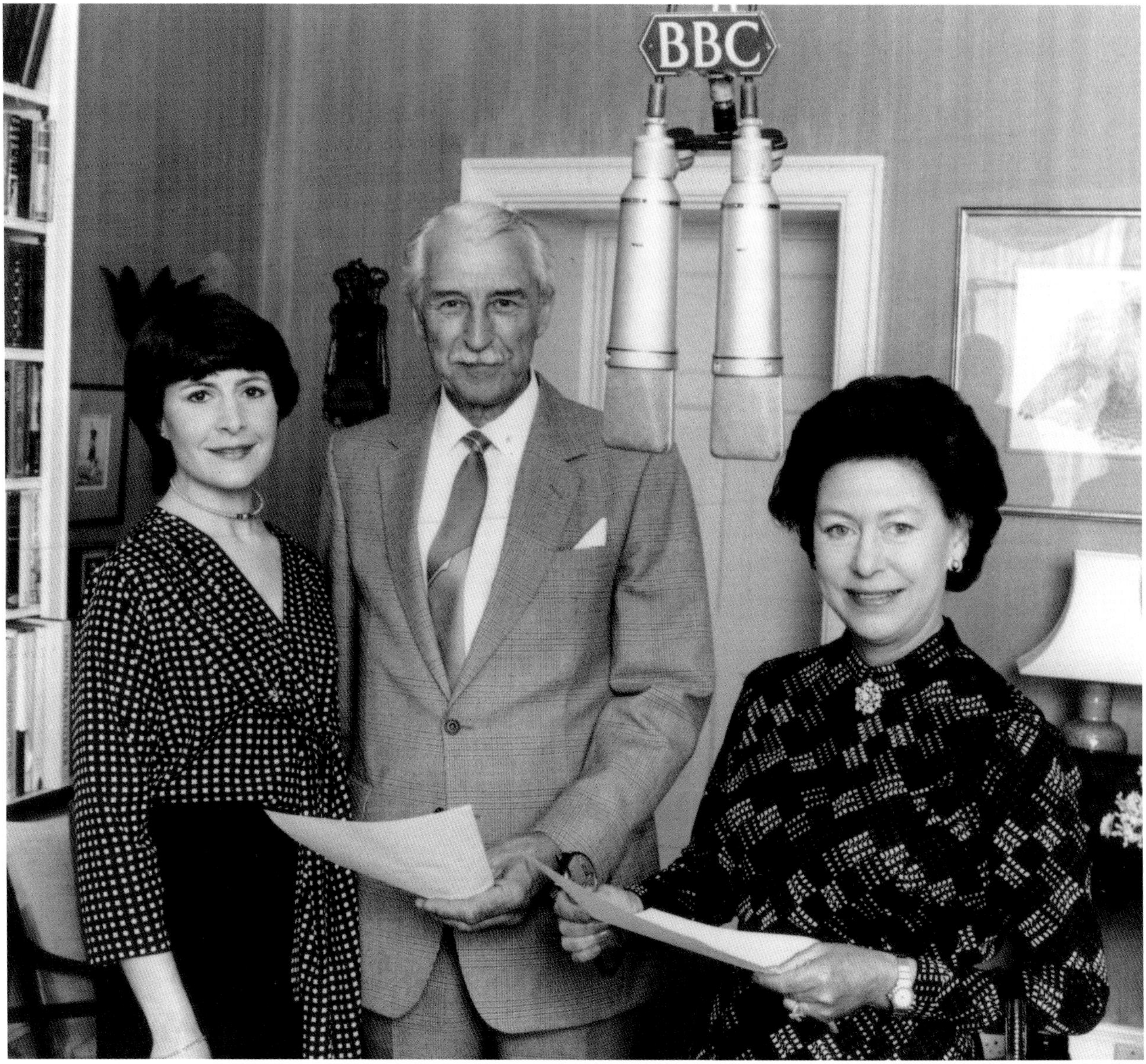
BBC

JULY

WEEK 30
2009

20 Monday — JAMIE PERKS BORN 1995

21 Tuesday

22 Wednesday — *New Moon*

23 Thursday

24 Friday

25 Saturday

26 Sunday — SIPHO MADIKANE BORN 2007

CAROLINE BONE (SARA COWARD), JACK WOOLLEY (ARNOLD PETERS) WITH HRH PRINCESS MARGARET

JULY | AUGUST

WEEK 31
2009

27 Monday

28 Tuesday *First Quarter*

29 Wednesday

30 Thursday

31 Friday

1 Saturday

2 Sunday

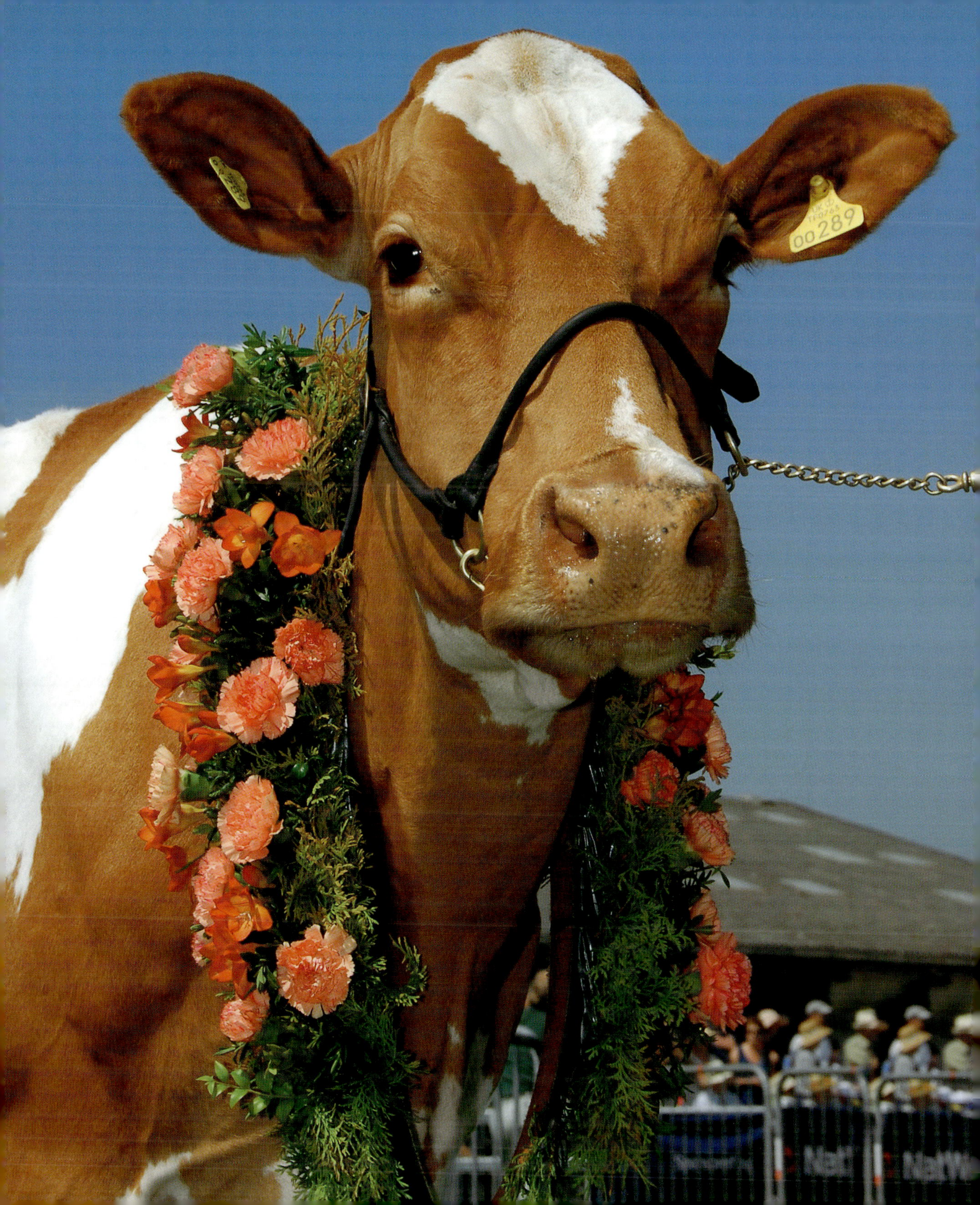
00289

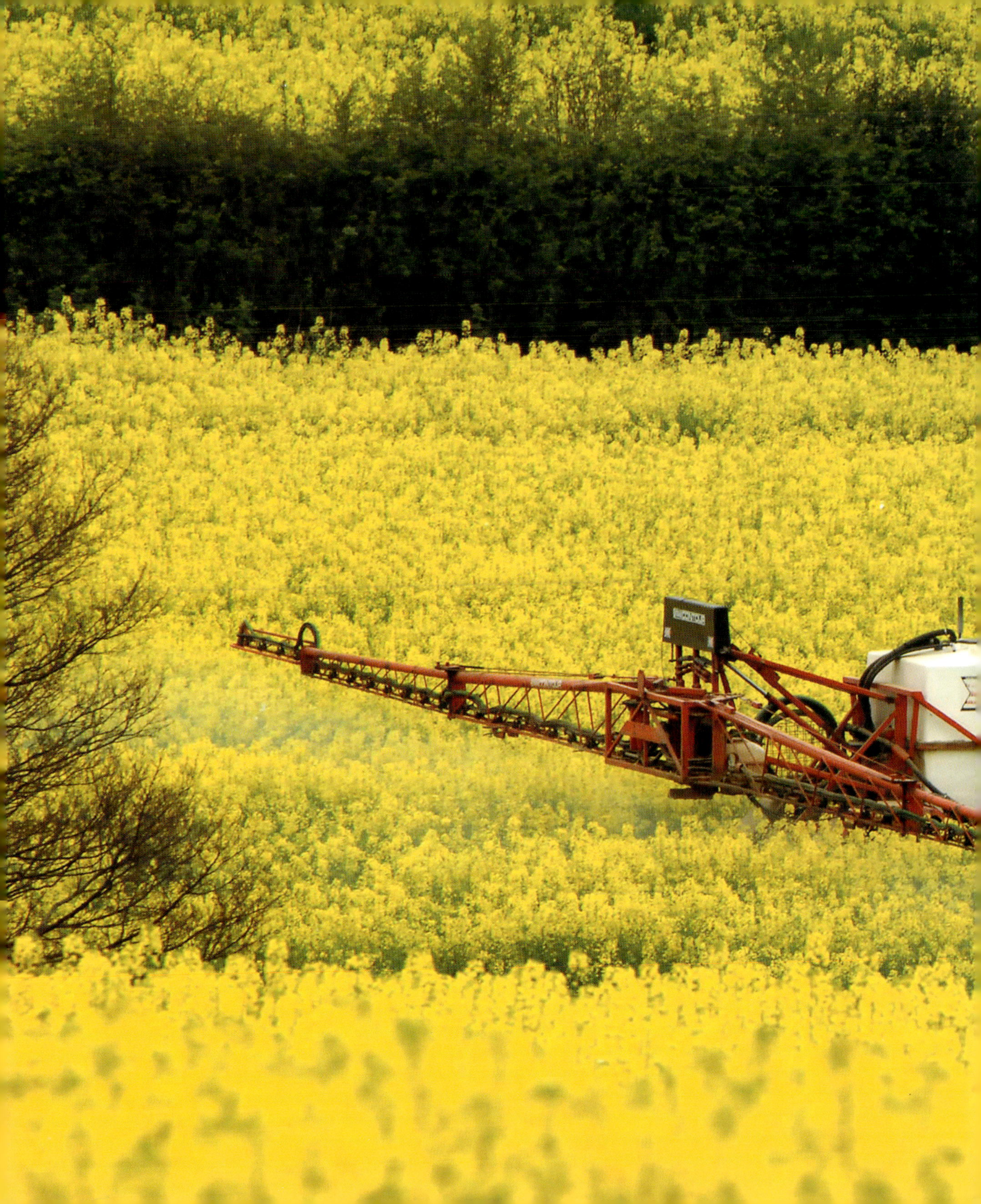

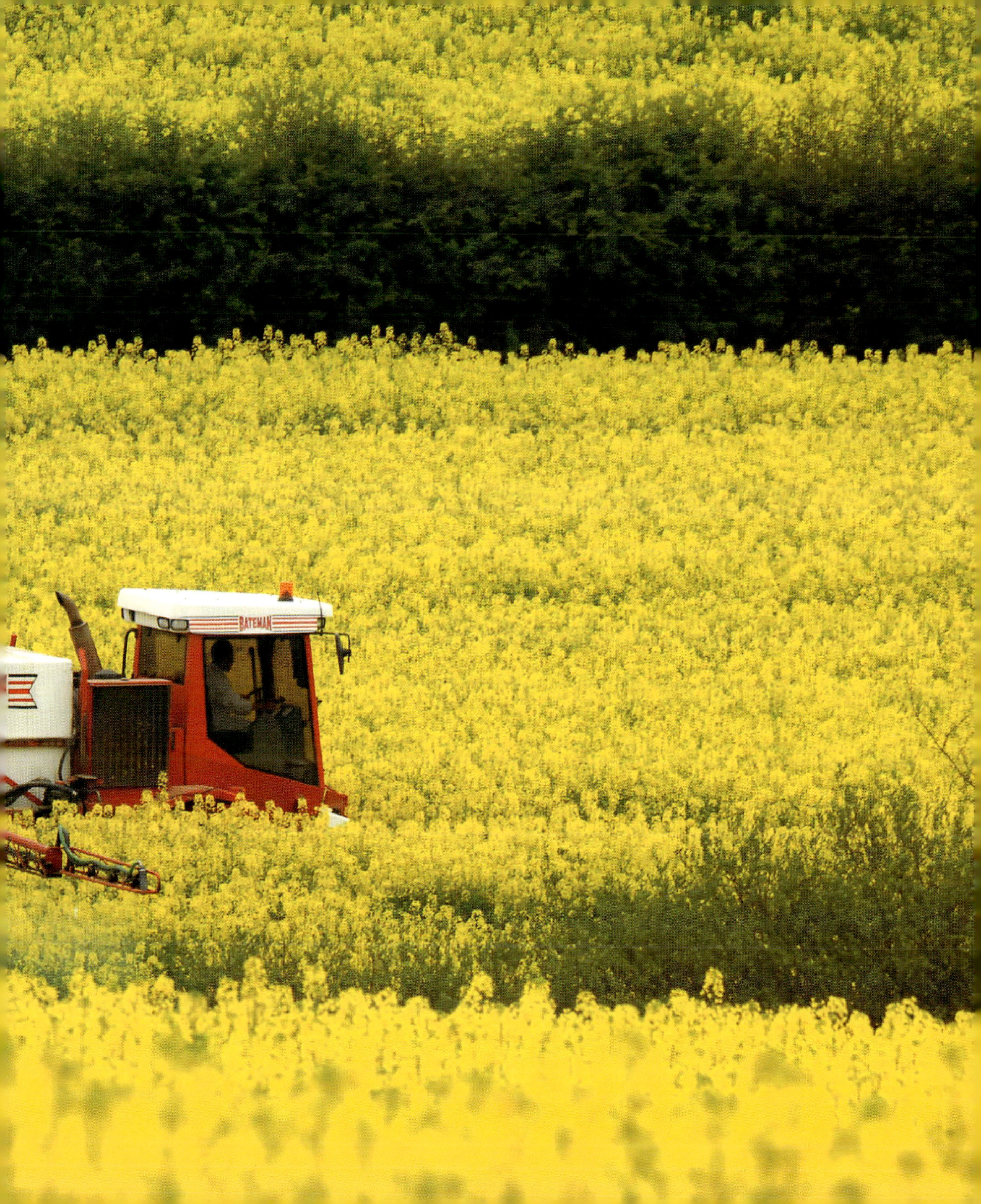
BATEMAN

AUGUST

WEEK 32
2009

3 Monday — Summer Bank Holiday, Scotland
Holiday, Republic of Ireland

4 Tuesday

5 Wednesday

6 Thursday — *Full Moon*

7 Friday — EMMA GRUNDY BORN 1984
MATT CRAWFORD BORN 1947

8 Saturday — SHULA HEBDEN-LLOYD AND KENTON ARCHER BORN 1958

9 Sunday

AUGUST

WEEK 33
2009

10 Monday

11 Tuesday

12 Wednesday

13 Thursday *Last Quarter*

14 Friday

15 Saturday

16 Sunday

GREY GABLES

THE PROOF'S IN THE PUDDING!
IAN'S STRAWBERRY GRANITA

Those long-term listeners among us will fondly remember Jean-Paul Aubert - the wonderful French chef notorious for his forthright manner and perfectionist approach to cooking. He brought excellence to the Grey Gables kitchen before passing on the mantle to Ian Craig who continues to delight clientele with his top-notch cooking. Here's one of Ian's favourite recipes, using fresh strawberries from Adam.

Serves 8

INGREDIENTS

450g (1lb) ripe strawberries
175g (6oz) caster sugar
570ml (1 pint) water
3 tbsp lemon juice

You will also need a polythene freezer box 20 x 20cm x 6cm deep (8 x 8in x 2½in) deep

METHOD

- Hull strawberries and rinse.
- Drain well, dry with kitchen roll, and put in a food processor.
- Blend into a smooth purée, add sugar and blend briefly.
- Add water and lemon juice and blend again.
- Sieve mixture then pour into freezer box. Cover and freeze for 2 hours.
- Stir the semi-frozen mixture thoroughly with a fork and freeze for 1 hour.
- Repeat the previous step. Mixture is now ready to serve and will stay the right consistency for 3–4 hours in the freezer.
- Spoon into wine glasses to see your dessert sparkle, and garnish with a sprig of mint.

☆ IAN'S TOP TIP ☆

"We serve this dessert in the restaurant, but it also makes a really refreshing end to a summer barbecue. To get your party going with a bang (or if Lilian's invited), substitute some of the water with a splash of triple sec and enjoy."

AUGUST

WEEK 34
2009

17 Monday　　　　　　　　　　　　　　　　　　　　　　　　JULIA PARGETTER-CARMICHAEL BORN 1924

18 Tuesday

19 Wednesday

20 Thursday　　　　　　　　　　　　　　　　　　　　　　　　　　　　　　　　　*New Moon*

21 Friday

22 Saturday　　　　　　　　　　　　　　　　First day of Ramadân (subject to sighting of the moon)

23 Sunday

AUGUST

WEEK 35
2009

24 Monday

25 Tuesday

26 Wednesday

27 Thursday

First Quarter
EMMA AND WILLIAM GRUNDY MARRIED 2004

28 Friday

29 Saturday

30 Sunday

EDWARD AND WILLIAM GRUNDY (BARRY FARRIMOND AND PHILIP MOLLOY)

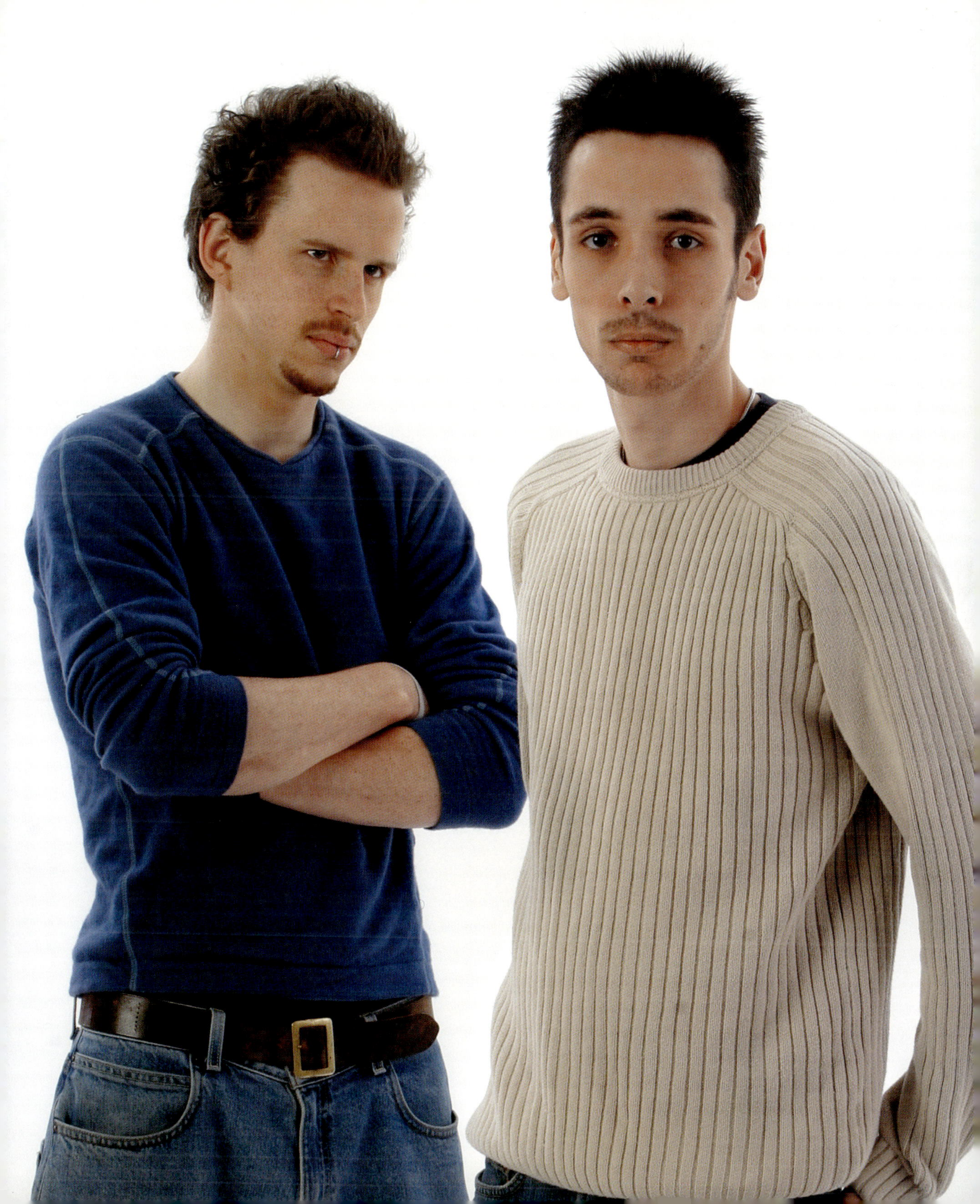

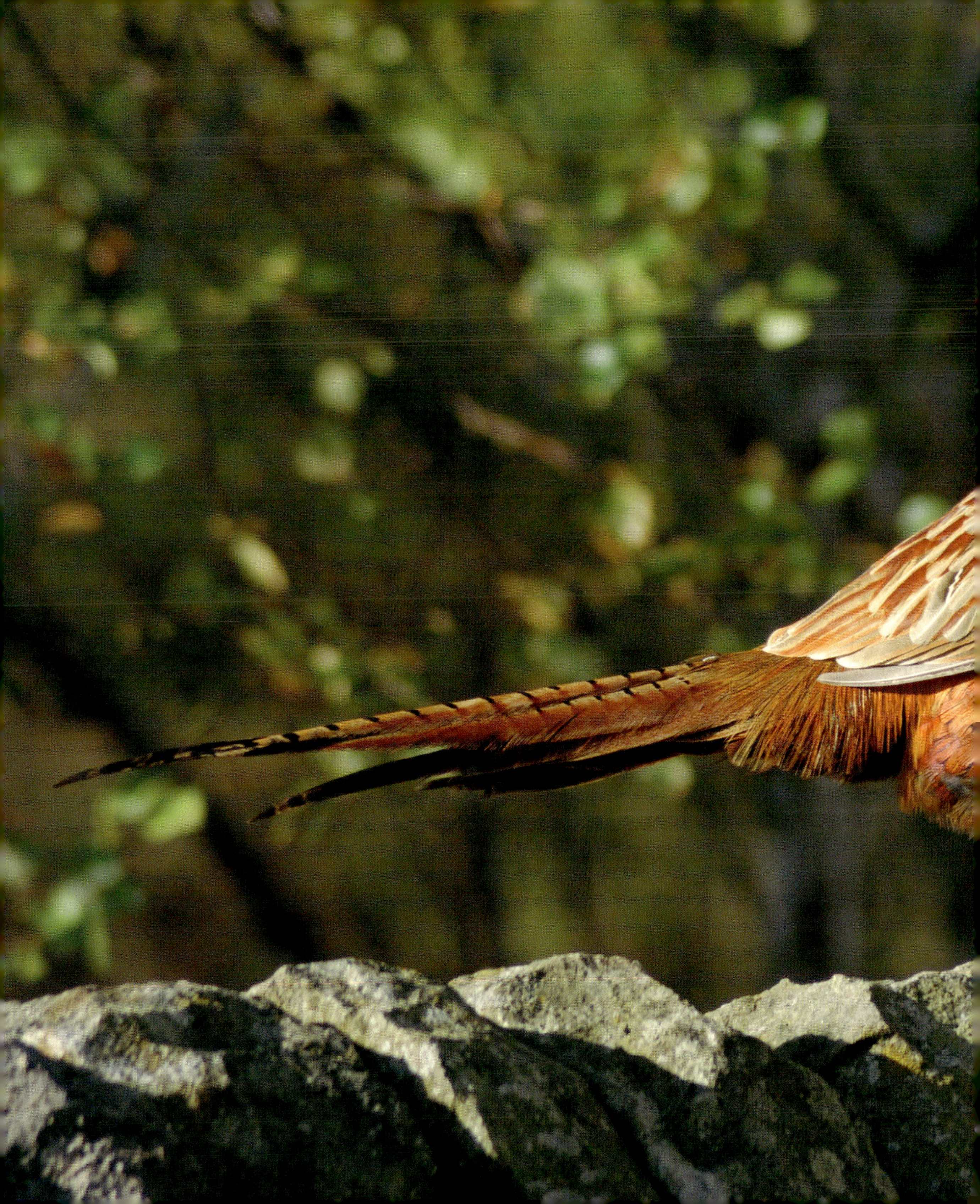

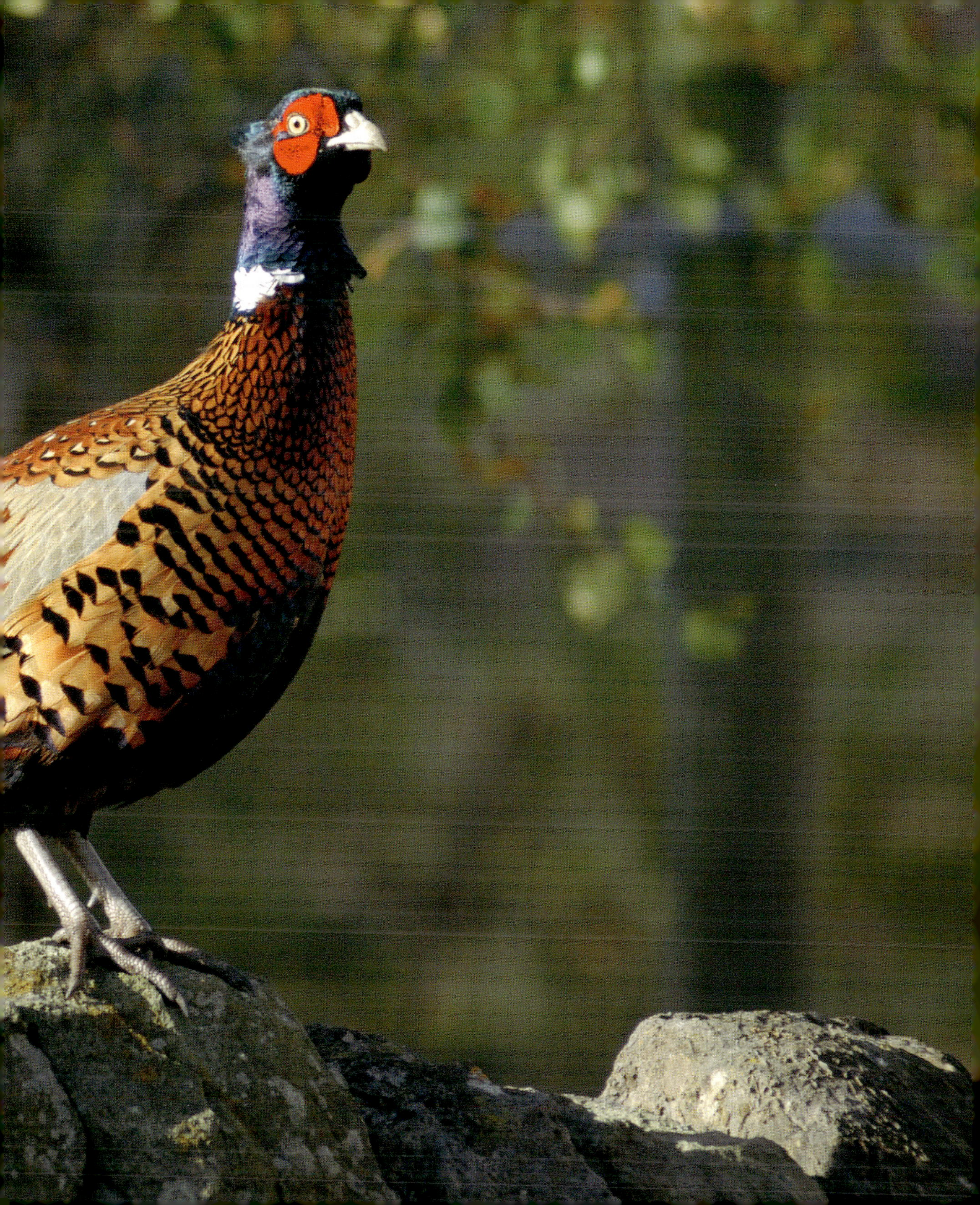

AUGUST | SEPTEMBER

WEEK 36
2009

31 Monday Summer Bank Holiday, UK exc. Scotland

1 Tuesday

2 Wednesday

3 Thursday LILIAN AND RALPH BELLAMY MARRIED 1971

4 Friday *Full Moon*

5 Saturday

6 Sunday Father's Day, Australia and New Zealand

SEPTEMBER

WEEK 37
2009

7 Monday   Holiday, USA (Labor Day)
                                          Holiday, Canada (Labour Day)

8 Tuesday

9 Wednesday

10 Thursday

11 Friday   CAROLINE AND GUY PEMBERTON MARRIED 1995

12 Saturday   *Last Quarter*

13 Sunday   JOSH ARCHER BORN 1997

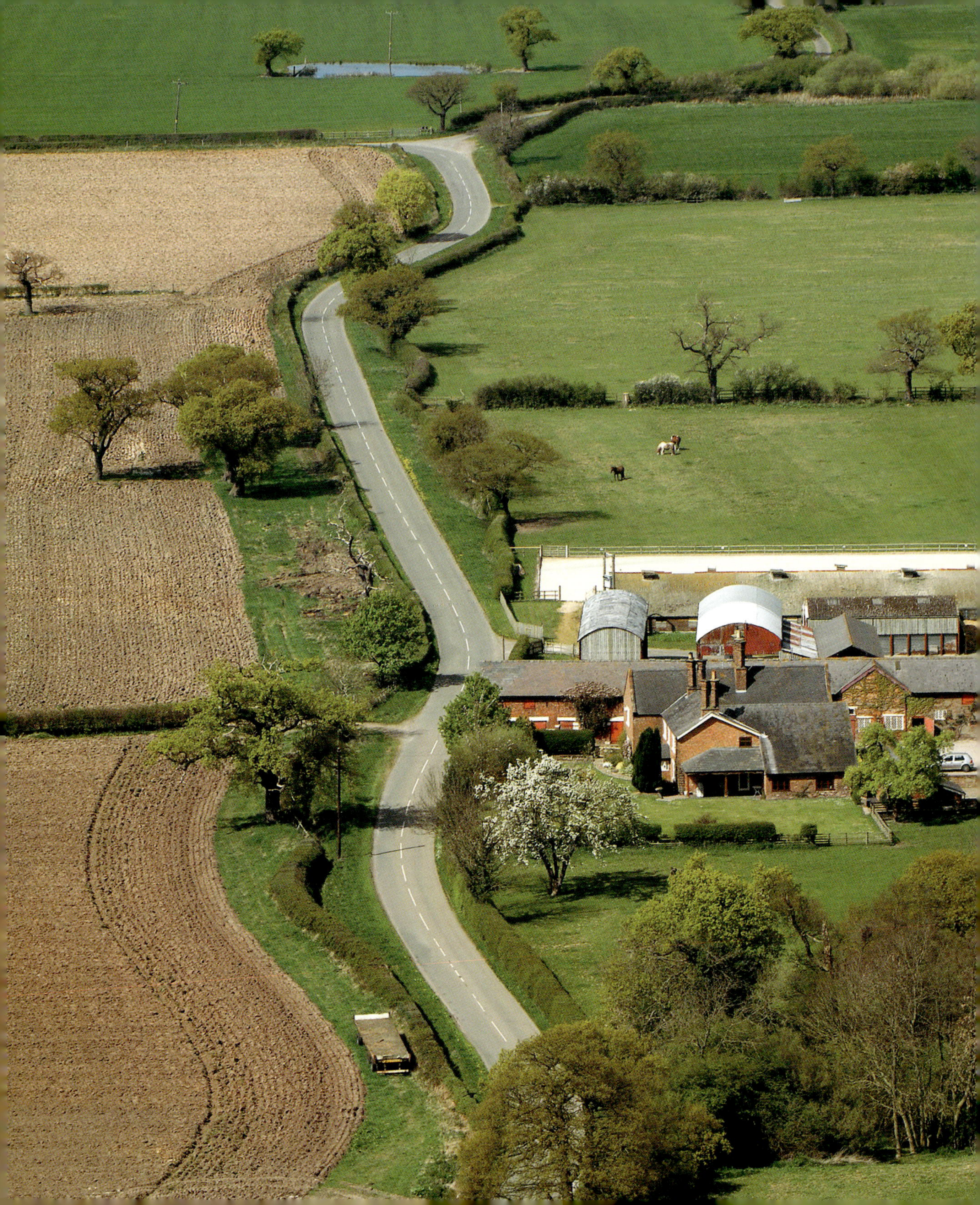

SEPTEMBER

WEEK 38
2009

14 Monday

15 Tuesday

16 Wednesday

17 Thursday

18 Friday

New Moon
JOE GRUNDY BORN 1921
DAVID ARCHER BORN 1959

19 Saturday

Jewish New Year (Rosh Hashanah)

20 Sunday

SEPTEMBER

WEEK 39
2009

21 Monday

Eid al Fitr, Ramadân ends
SHULA AND MARK HEBDEN MARRIED 1985

22 Tuesday

Autumnal Equinox
GRACE ARCHER DIED 1955

23 Wednesday

24 Thursday

25 Friday

26 Saturday

First Quarter

27 Sunday

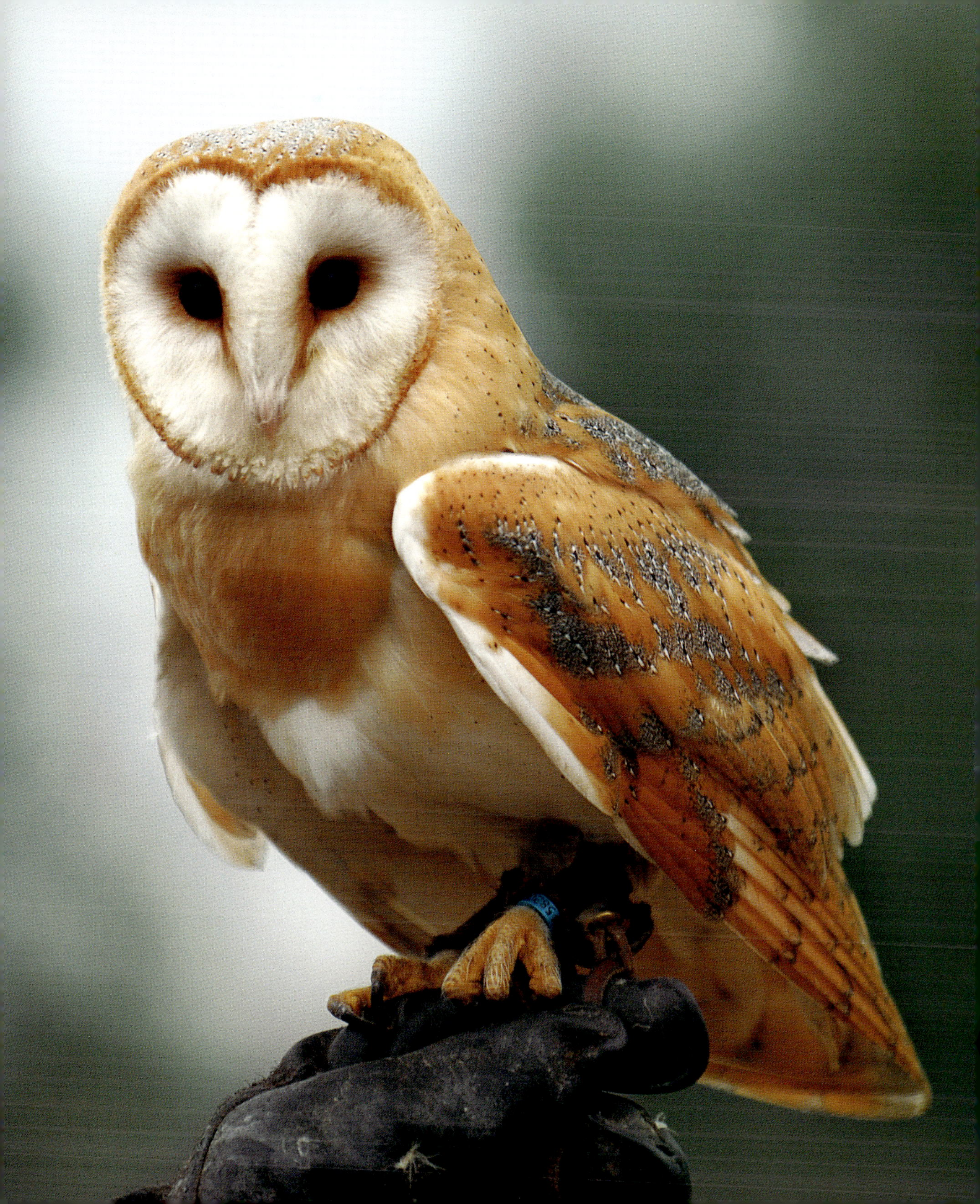

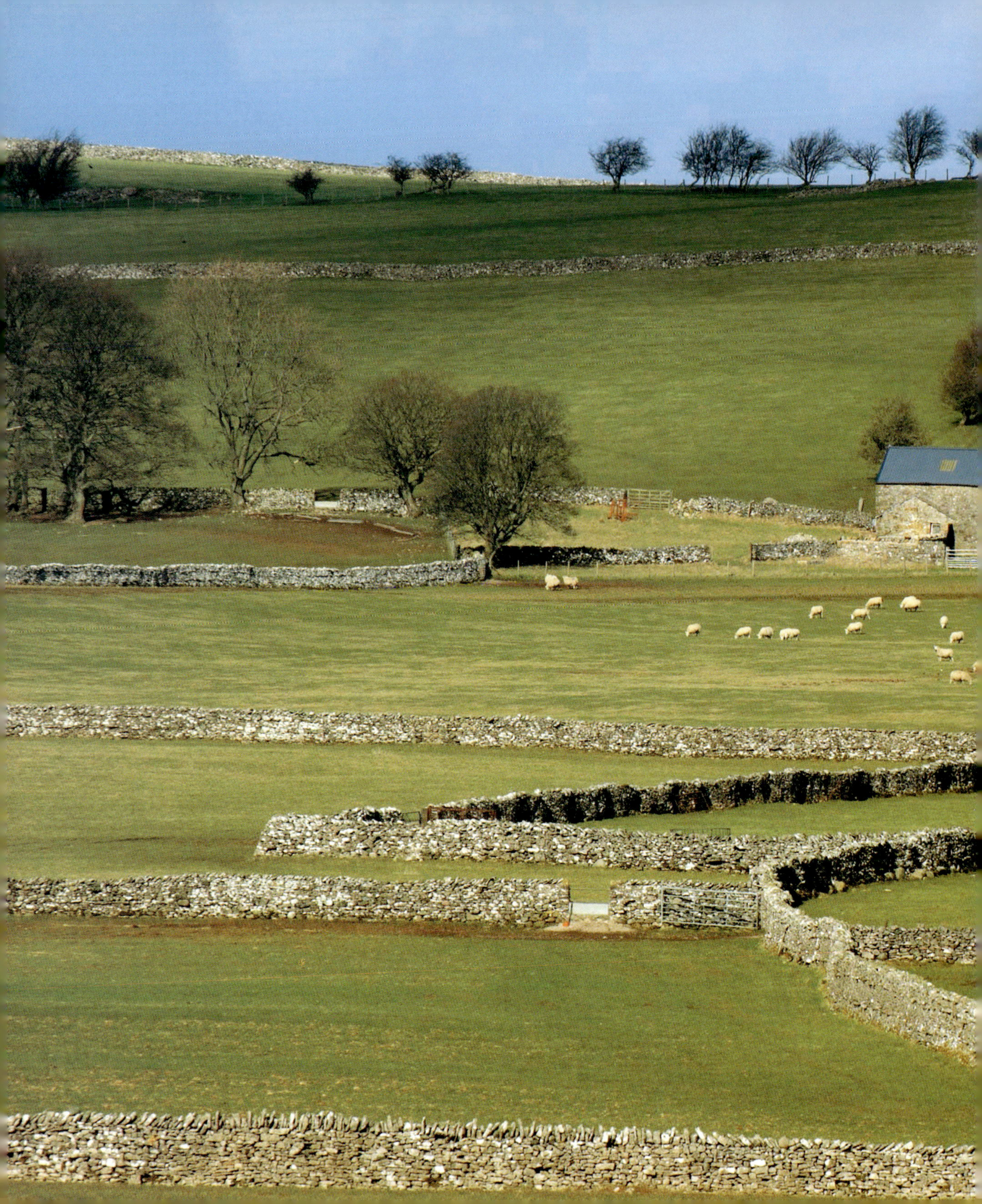

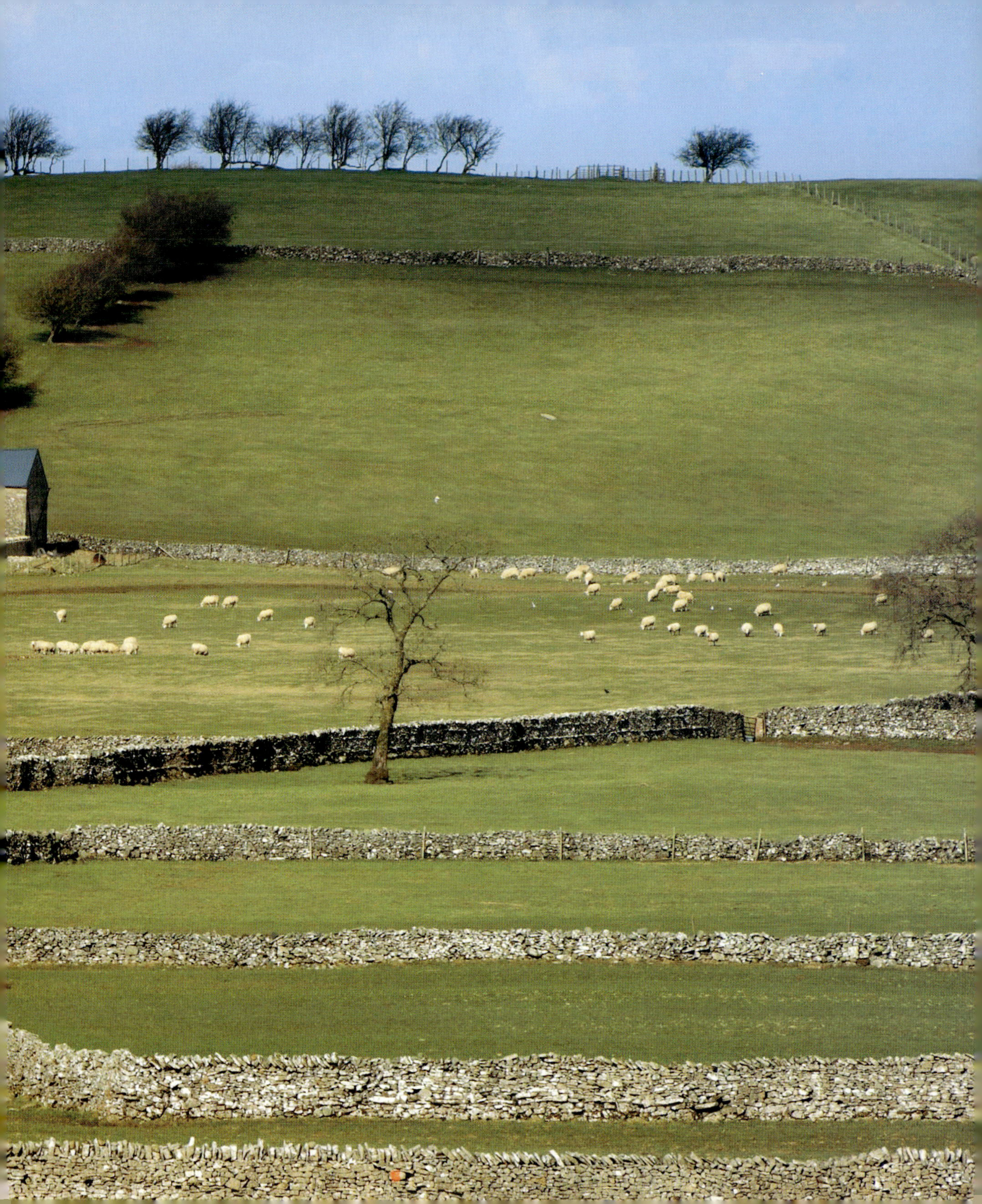

SEPTEMBER | OCTOBER

WEEK 40
2009

28 Monday

Day of Atonement (Yom Kippur)
EDWARD GRUNDY BORN 1984

29 Tuesday

Michaelmas Day
ALICE ALDRIDGE BORN 1988
ELIZABETH AND NIGEL PARGETTER MARRIED 1994

30 Wednesday

KATE MADIKANE BORN 1977

1 Thursday

OMNIBUS FIRST HEARD ON RADIO 4 1967

2 Friday

GODFREY BASELY, CREATOR OF *THE ARCHERS*, BORN 1904
FIRST DAILY EPISODES ON RADIO 4 1967

3 Saturday

Festival of Tabernacles (Succoth), First Day
JILL ARCHER BORN 1930

4 Sunday

Full Moon

OCTOBER

WEEK 41
2009

5 Monday

6 Tuesday

7 Wednesday

8 Thursday

9 Friday

10 Saturday   Festival of Tabernacles (Succoth), Eighth Day
                              SUSAN CARTER BORN 1963

11 Sunday   *Last Quarter*

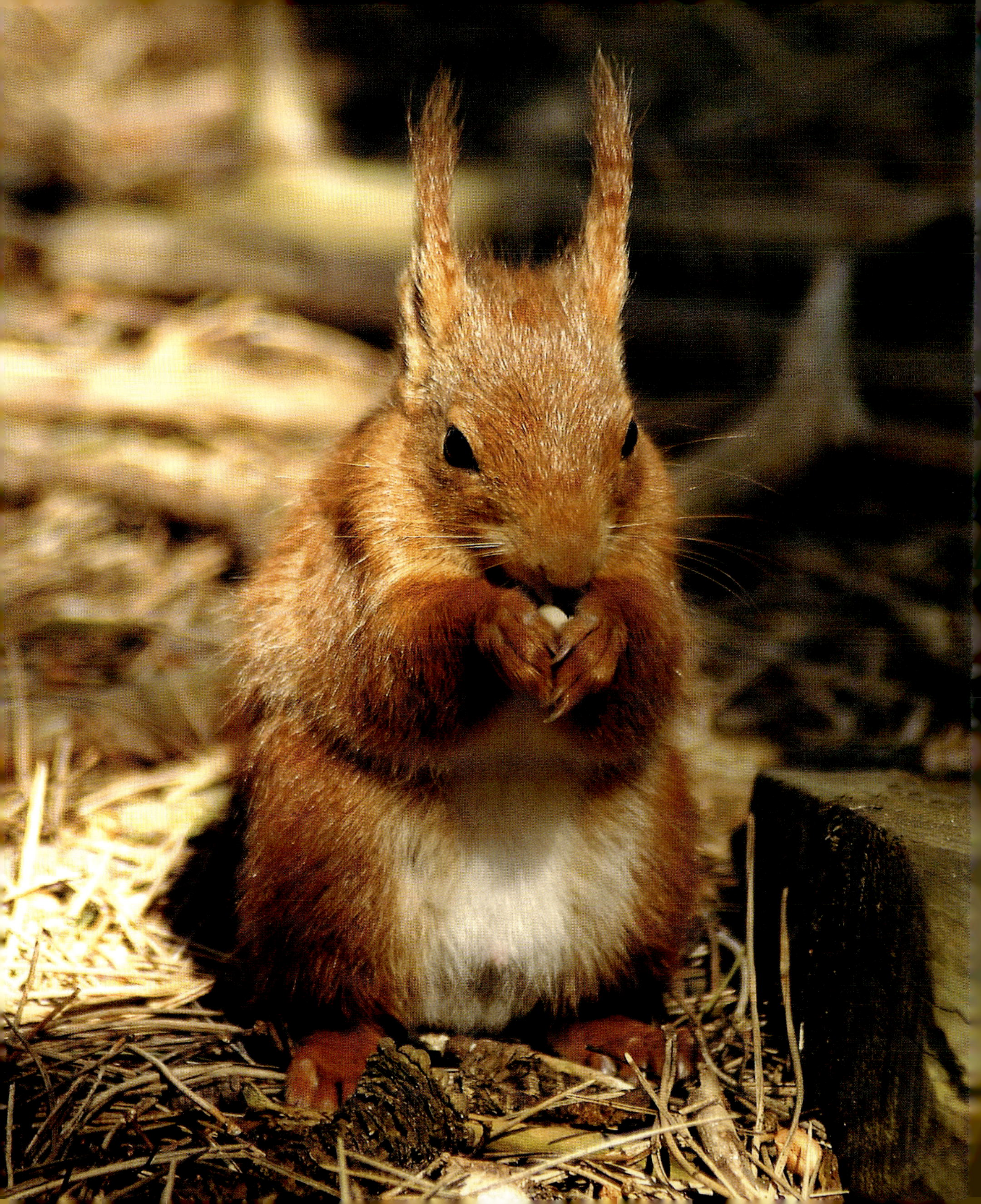

OCTOBER

WEEK 42
2009

12 Monday
Holiday, Canada (Thanksgiving)
Holiday, USA (Columbus Day)

13 Tuesday

14 Wednesday

15 Thursday

16 Friday

17 Saturday

18 Sunday
New Moon
ARCHERS ADDICTS FOUNDED

OCTOBER

WEEK 43
2009

19 Monday

20 Tuesday

21 Wednesday

22 Thursday

23 Friday

24 Saturday

United Nations Day
GEORGE BARFORD BORN 1928
FIRST EPISODE FROM THE MAILBOX BROADCAST 2004

25 Sunday

British Summer Time ends
DORIS ARCHER DIED 1980

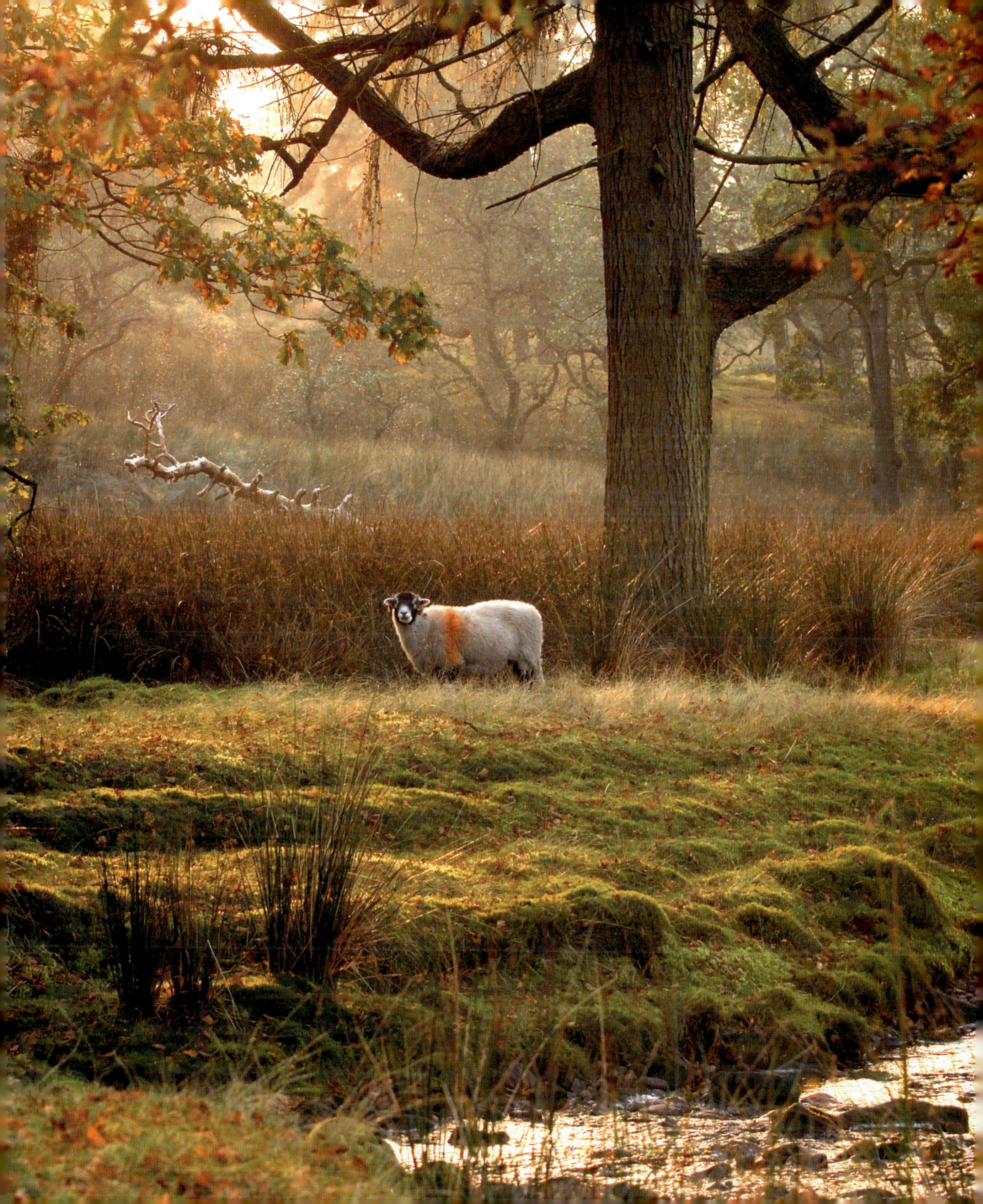

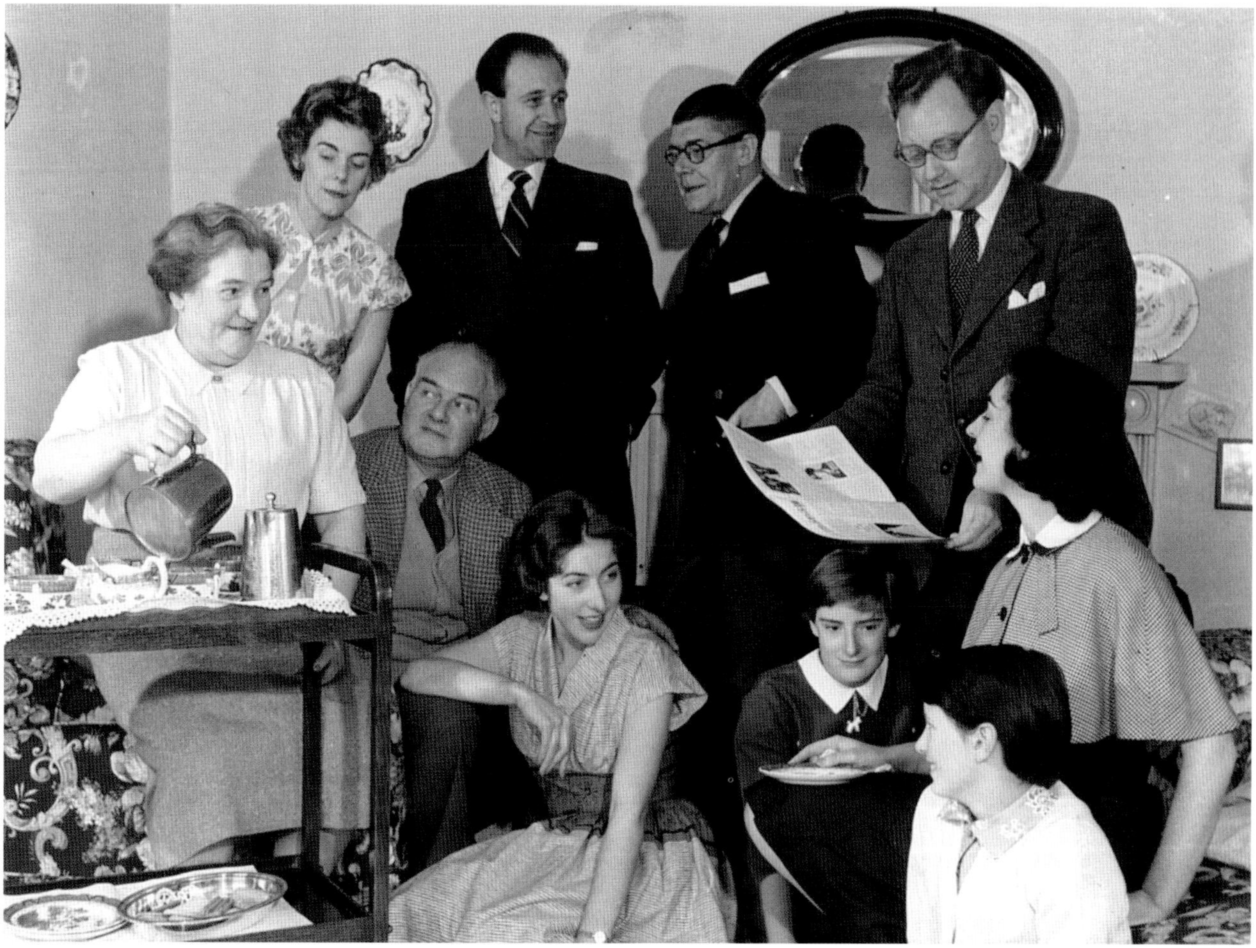

OCTOBER | NOVEMBER

WEEK 44
2009

26 Monday
Holiday, New Zealand (Labour Day)
Holiday, Republic of Ireland
First Quarter

27 Tuesday

28 Wednesday

29 Thursday

30 Friday

31 Saturday
Hallowe'en

1 Sunday
All Saints' Day

DORIS ARCHER (GWEN BERRYMAN) PRESIDES OVER TEA-TIME AT BROOKFIELD, 1958

AMBRIDGE LANDMARKS
Lakey Hill

THE DETAILS:

Location: 771 feet (235 meters) above sea level to the north-east of Ambridge

Age: As old as the hills! Traces of several prehistoric burial mounds

Facilities: Lakey Hill offers a stunning view of the Borsetshire countryside and some welcome respite from nosy neighbours and the hustle and bustle of busy village life.

Owners: As part of the Brookfield Estate, the summit and lower slopes are owned by the Archer family.

OVER THE HILL:

Overlooking the picturesque village of Ambridge, the rolling slopes of Lakey Hill reflect the ups and downs of life for the residents of Ambridge. While its gentle slopes have provided a calm place for reflection and quiet contemplation, they have also witnessed some emotional events, from courtship to criminal offences. It is no surprise, then, that in 2007 Phil decided to take Jill to the top of Lakey Hill to celebrate their golden wedding anniversary. There he presented her with an eternity ring and they chatted together overlooking the village. Did he think back to 1953 when he sat there with his first wife, Grace, as they roasted potatoes in the remains of the Coronation Day bonfire?

No matter what dramas unfold on its grassy gradients, Lakey Hill stands tall and quiet as a testament to the longevity of Ambridge and the peace of life in the countryside. As part of the Brookfield Estate, the farm's lambs continue to graze on its lower slopes – let's hope they appreciate the view!

IF WALLS HAD EARS…

- …they'd blush to hear Mark Hebden propose to Shula on New Years Eve 1985, and when Elizabeth accepted a proposal from Nigel (second time lucky) atop Lakey Hill.

- …The soil hasn't always been so fertile (!), and some expletives will have been heard when Phil struggled to plough the top field, only to stall the tractor and injure himself.

- …Lakey Hill also led to misfortune for George Fairbrother in 1956 when he burnt off gorse and heather without a licence – he was fined £2 for arson.

Pictured right: Ruth and David Archer (Felicity Finch and Timothy Bentinck).

SOUNDBITE:
As you well know, it's hard to find privacy in Ambridge, so Lakey Hill has been the setting for many courting couples over the years. Actors used to kiss the back of their hands to simulate smooching but now, thanks to sensitive stereo recording techniques, the actors have to kiss each other… it's a tough job, but someone's got to do it! Elizabeth and Nigel Pargetter (Alison Dowling and Graham Seed) pictured right.

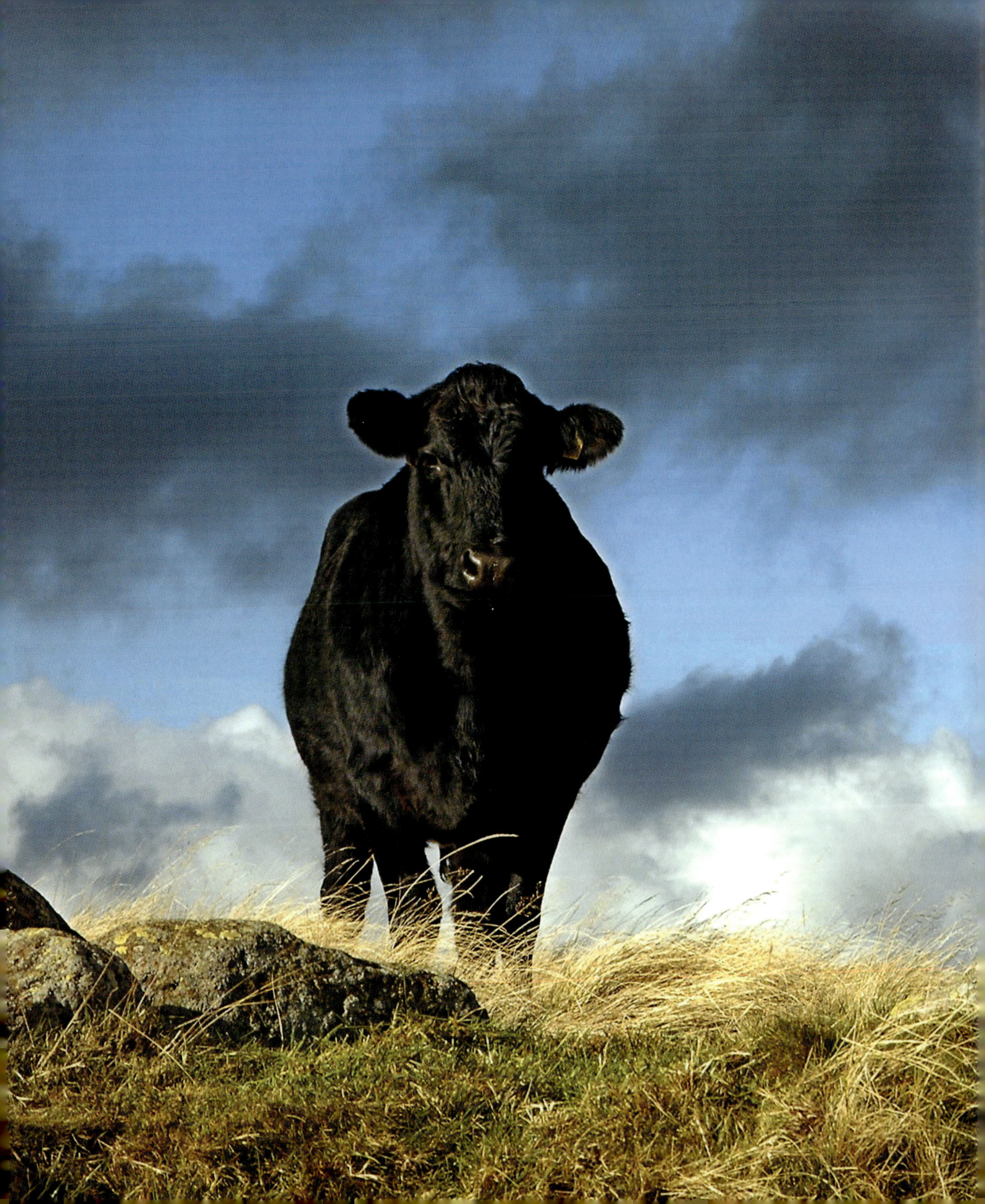

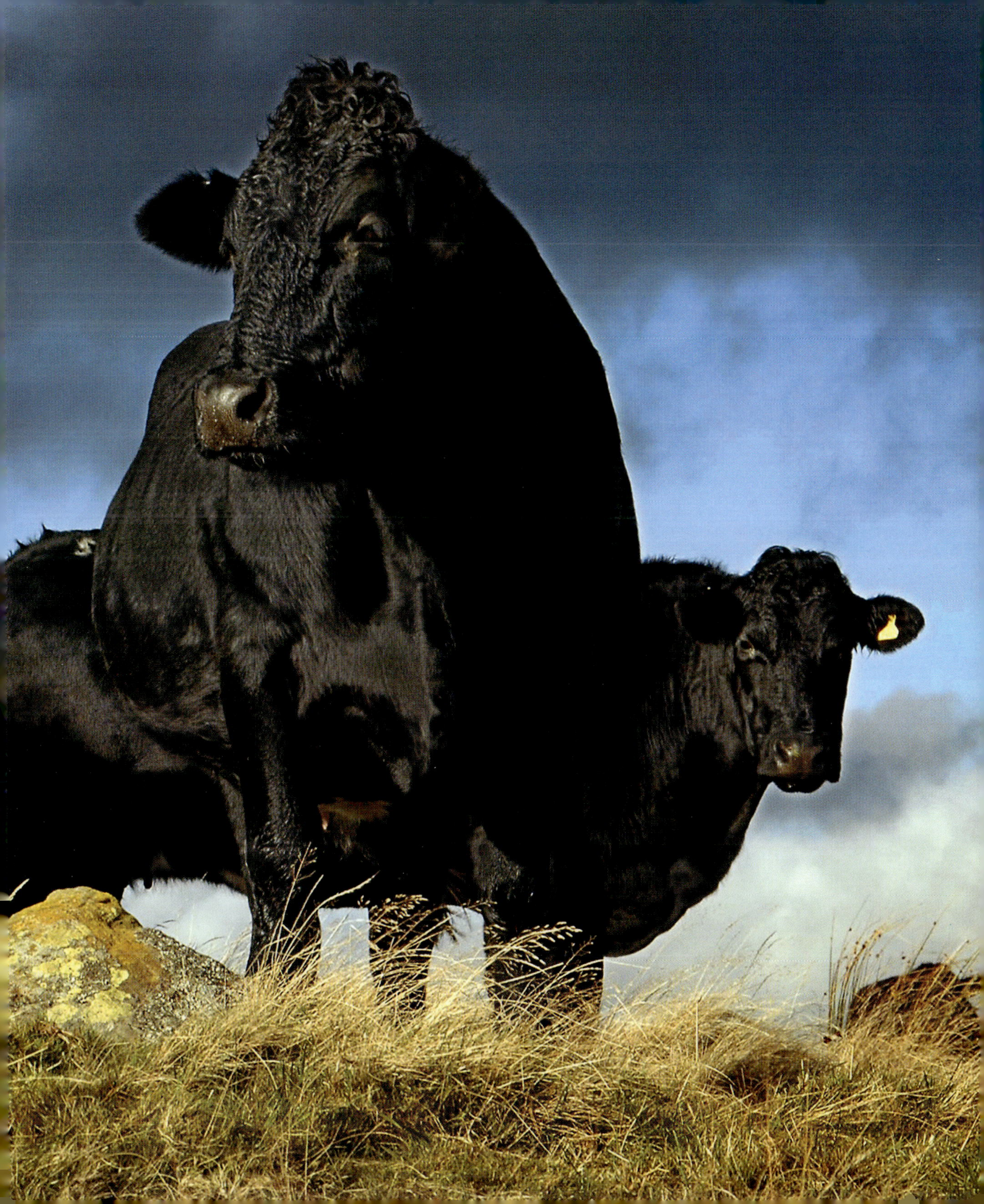

NOVEMBER

WEEK 45
2009

2 Monday *Full Moon*

3 Tuesday

4 Wednesday

5 Thursday Guy Fawkes' Day

6 Friday

7 Saturday JULIA CARMICHAEL-PARGETTER DIED 2005
15,000TH EPISODE BROADCAST 2006

8 Sunday Remembrance Sunday, UK

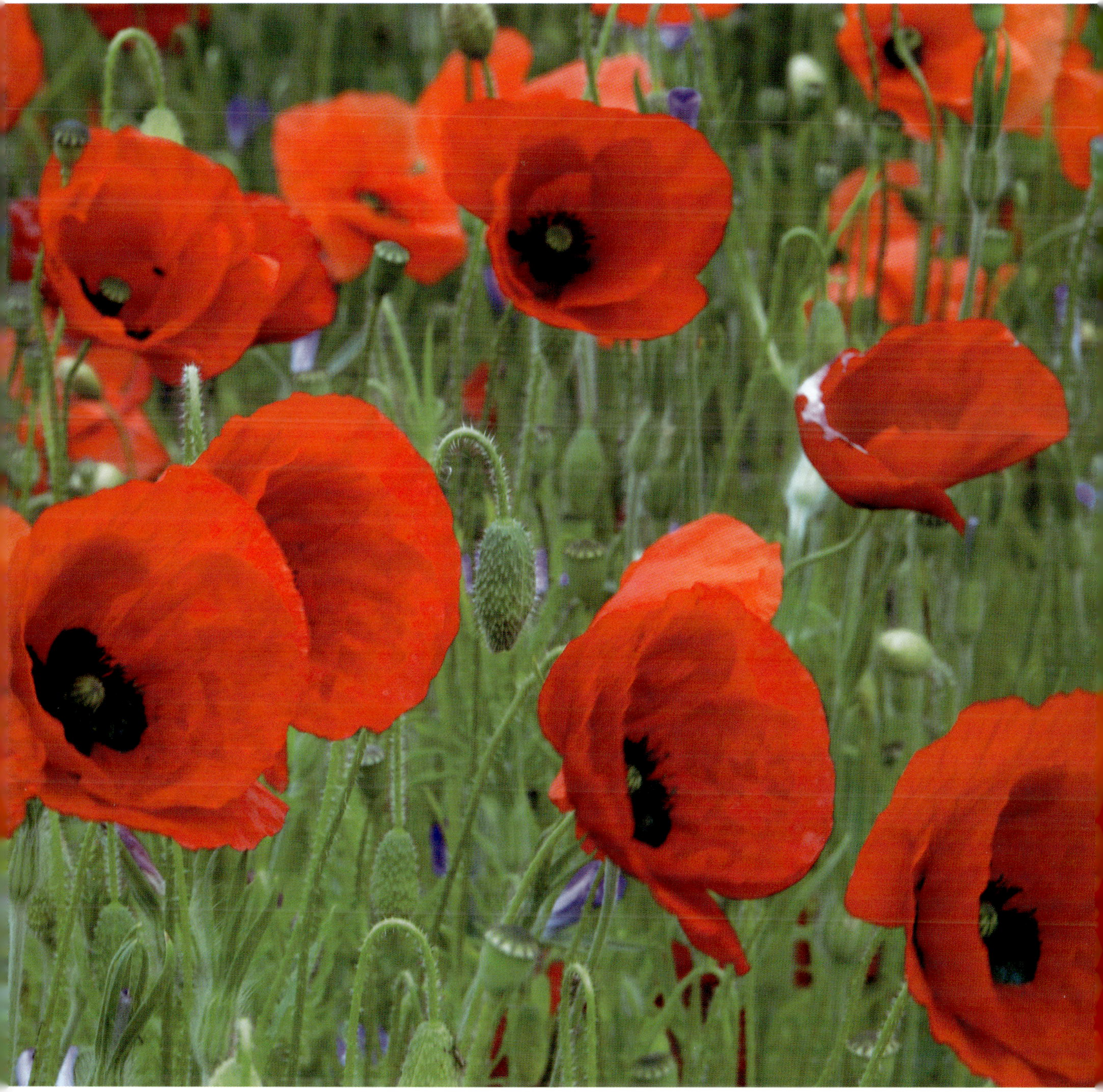

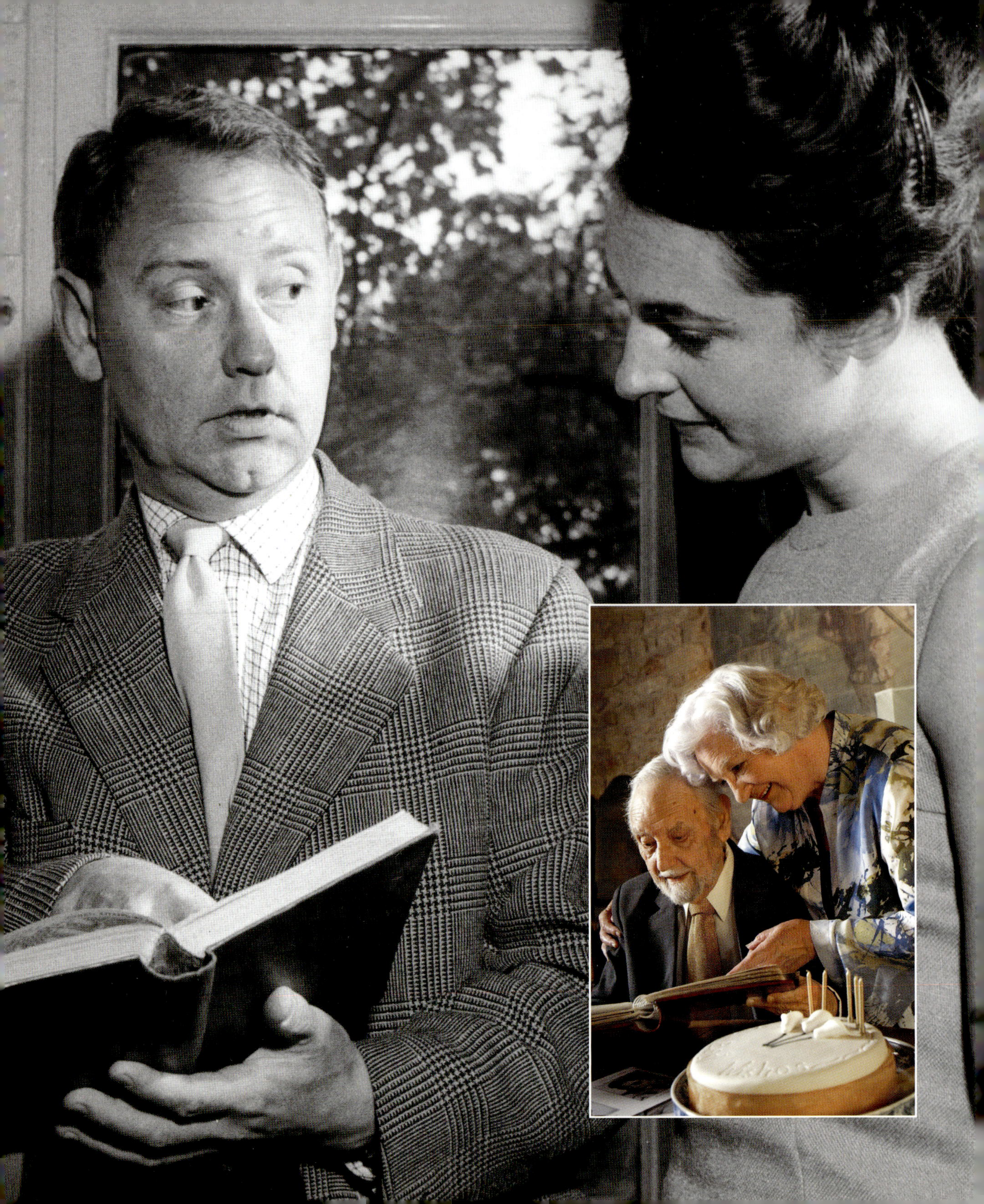

NOVEMBER

WEEK 46
2009

9 Monday *Last Quarter*

10 Tuesday

11 Wednesday   Holiday, USA (Veterans' Day)
Holiday, Canada (Remembrance Day)

12 Thursday

13 Friday   PEGGY WOOLLEY BORN 1924

14 Saturday   DANIEL HEBDEN-LLOYD BORN 1994
RUAIRI DONOVAN BORN 2002

15 Sunday

PHIL AND JILL ARCHER (NORMAN PAINTING AND PATRICIA GREENE) IN 1962, AND CELEBRATING THEIR GOLDEN WEDDING ANNIVERSAY IN 2007

NOVEMBER

WEEK 47
2009

16 Monday
New Moon
JILL AND PHIL ARCHER MARRIED 1957

17 Tuesday

18 Wednesday

19 Thursday
THE ARCHERS FIRST BROADCAST ON THE INTERNET 1999

20 Friday
BRIAN ALDRIDGE BORN 1943

21 Saturday
CLARRIE AND EDDIE GRUNDY MARRIED 1981

22 Sunday

NOVEMBER

WEEK 48
2009

23 Monday

24 Tuesday *First Quarter*

25 Wednesday

26 Thursday Holiday, USA (Thanksgiving Day)

27 Friday

28 Saturday

29 Sunday First Sunday in Advent

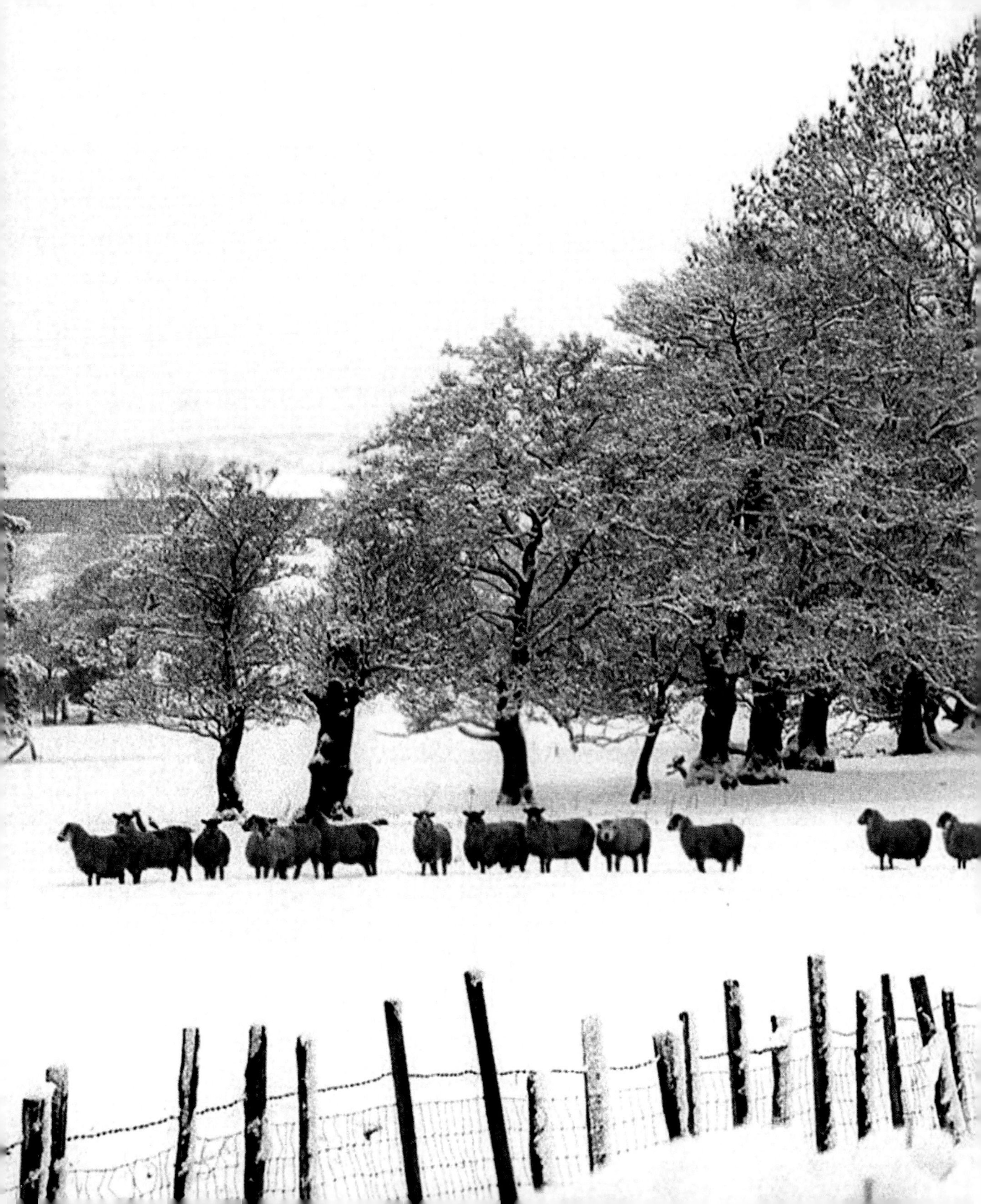

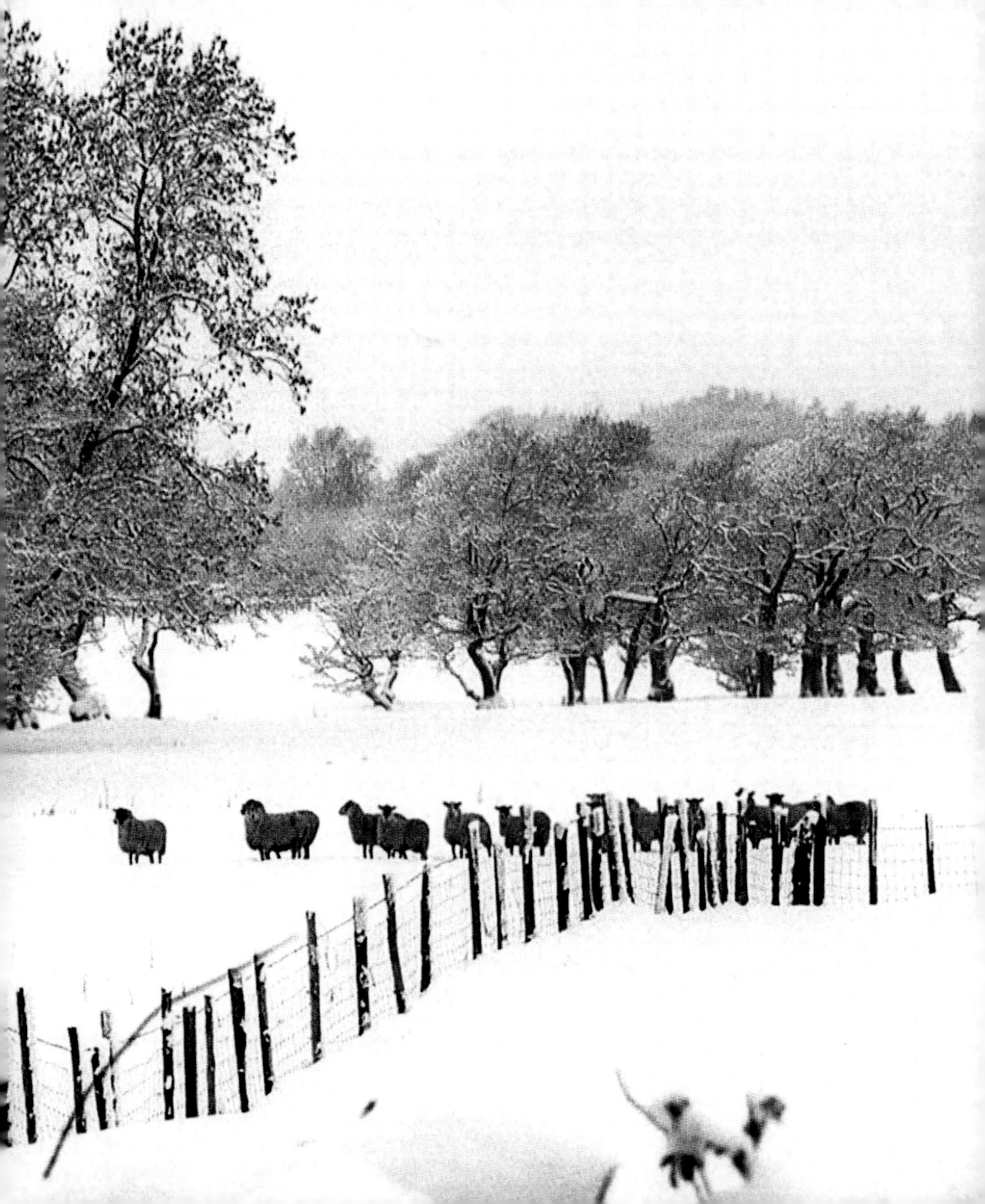

NOVEMBER | DECEMBER

WEEK 49
2009

30 Monday — St. Andrew's Day

1 Tuesday — MIKE TUCKER BORN 1949

2 Wednesday — *Full Moon*

3 Thursday

4 Friday

5 Saturday

6 Sunday

DECEMBER

WEEK 50
2009

7 Monday

8 Tuesday

9 Wednesday									*Last Quarter*

10 Thursday

11 Friday

12 Saturday					Jewish Festival of Chanukah, First Day
						LUCY GEMMELL BORN 1971
					PAT AND TONY ARCHER MARRIED 1974
					LILY AND FREDDIE PARGETTER BORN 1999

13 Sunday

DECEMBER

WEEK 51
2009

14 Monday   ADAM MACY AND IAN CRAIG CIVIL PARTNERSHIP 2006

15 Tuesday   RUTH AND DAVID ARCHER MARRIED 1988

16 Wednesday   *New Moon*
                                                              BETTY TUCKER DIED 2005

17 Thursday

18 Friday   Islamic New Year (subject to sighting of the moon)

19 Saturday

20 Sunday

LAKEY HILL

LUSCIOUS LAMB
RUTH'S SIMPLE SUPPER

Lakey Hill is enjoyed by many ramblers and villagers seeking a moment of peace or a fabulous view. Since the hill was absorbed into the Brookfield estate, it also provides valuable grazing for the Hassett Hills lambs who forage on its lower slopes. Here's a recipe that is best cooked with fresh organic free range lamb.

Serves 4

INGREDIENTS

8 Hassett Hills lamb loin chops
1 small onion, chopped
watercress

For the sauce:
1 large onion, finely chopped
1tbsp rosemary leaves
25g (1oz) butter
25g (1oz) plain flour
175ml (6fl oz) milk
175ml (6fl oz) vegetable stock
2tbsp double cream

METHOD

- Preheat oven to Gas Mark 6, (200°C) and roast lamb chops and onion in shallow roasting tin on top shelf for 30 minutes for pink (45 minutes if you like them well-done).
- Meanwhile, melt butter in a saucepan and gently cook onions for 5 minutes.
- Chop rosemary and add to onions. Cook gently for further 15 minutes.
- Stir in flour with wooden spoon, then gradually add milk then stock, stirring vigorously then whisking.
- Season and let sauce simmer for a couple of minutes.
- Serve drizzled over lamb with watercress to garnish.

☆ RUTH'S TOP TIP ☆

"If you've got picky children who don't like 'lumps', liquidise half of the sauce then mix it all together again before serving for a smoother gravy."

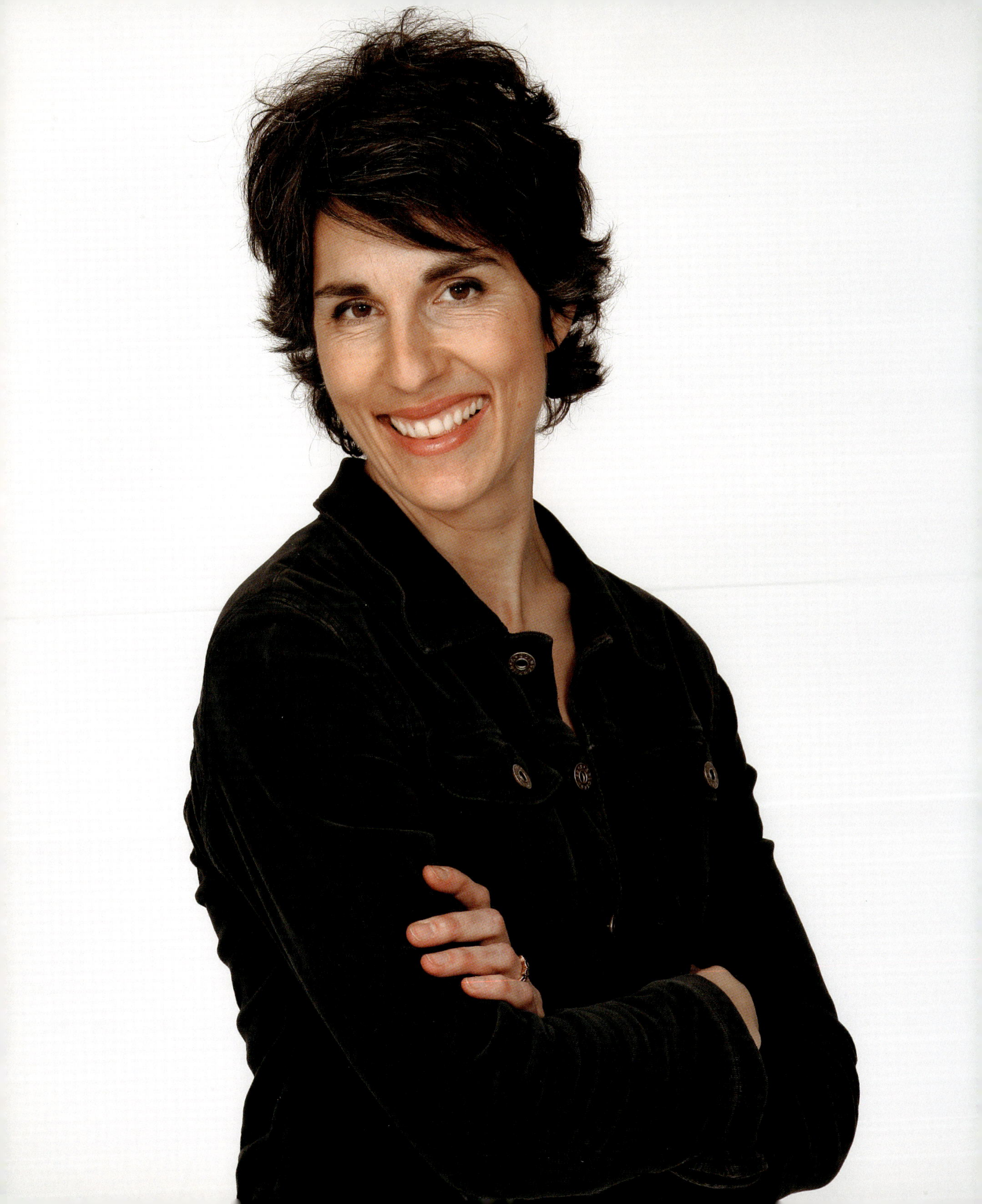

DECEMBER

WEEK 52
2009

21 Monday
Winter Solstice
CHRISTINE BARFORD BORN 1931

22 Tuesday

23 Wednesday

24 Thursday
Christmas Eve
First Quarter
DEBBIE ALDRIDGE BORN 1970
SHULA AND ALISTAIR LLOYD MARRIED 1998

25 Friday
Christmas Day
Holiday, UK, Republic of Ireland, Canada, USA,
Australia and New Zealand

26 Saturday
Boxing Day (St. Stephen's Day)

27 Sunday

DEBBIE ALDRIDGE (TAMSIN GREIG)

DECEMBER | JANUARY

WEEK 1
2010

28 Monday

Holiday, UK and Canada
GODFREY BASELEY PRESENTED 'INTRODUCING *THE ARCHERS*' 1950

29 Tuesday

30 Wednesday

31 Thursday

New Year's Eve
Full Moon
JOHN ARCHER BORN 1975

1 Friday

New Year's Day
Holiday, UK, Republic of Ireland, Canada, USA, Australia and New Zealand
JACK AND PEGGY WOOLLEY MARRIED 1991
***THE ARCHERS* FIRST BROADCAST NATIONWIDE 1951**

2 Saturday

Holiday, Scotland and New Zealand

3 Sunday

NOTES

BORSETSHIRE BRAINTEASERS – SOLUTIONS

RAMBLING AMBRIDGE ANAGRAMS!
Saint Stephens
Lower Loxley
Grey Gables
Lakey Hill
The Bull
Brookfield Farm

LOST IN SPACE!
Grange Farm
Police House
Woodbine Cottage
Village Hall
Honeysuckle Cottage
Nightingale Farm
The Stables
Ambridge Hall
Keeper's Cottage
Willow Farm

GUESS WHO?
Sterling
Pargetter
Tucker
Archer
Franks
Carter
Grundy
Lloyd
Woolley
Perks

Ambridge